PN   West, Thomas Reed.
49
W42   Nature, community, &
        will

DATE			

NATURE, COMMUNITY, & WILL

A STUDY IN LITERARY AND SOCIAL THOUGHT

THOMAS R. WEST

UNIVERSITY OF MISSOURI PRESS

COLUMBIA

Library of Congress Cataloging in Publication Data

West, Thomas Reed.
    Nature, community, & will.

    1. Literature and morals.   I. Title.
PN49.W42   820'.9'38   75–44076
ISBN 0–8262–0196–2

TO C.

ACKNOWLEDGMENTS

In a more finished acknowledgment, I would be faced with sorting out the special kinds of help I have received with this book. But that would have involved weighings and distinctions I cannot manage among people to whom I am grateful. Let me simply say that for their criticism and suggestion, I wish to thank these friends: Sandra Burner and David Burner at the State University of New York at Stony Brook; Maxwell Bloomfield, Father Joseph Moody, Philip Raidt, Joseph Williman, Ruth Zeender, and John Zeender at the Catholic University of America; Joseph Hernon at the University of Massachusetts at Amherst; James Mooney at Rice; Alfred H. Jones of the United States Information Agency; Robert Glenn Wright at Michigan State University; Peter Fuss at the University of Missouri —St. Louis; and Catherine Callan West.

I feel also a connection and gratitude to the larger community I have worked within—and this means especially to students who have talked with me through many courses indirectly but importantly related to my topic.

CONTENTS

Preface

9

I

The Devices of Nature

George Fitzhugh and Thomas Carlyle

15

II

The Divided Consciousness

Allen Tate, John Crowe Ransom, Paul Elmer More

40

III

Nature and Artifice

Hannah Arendt, Theodore Roszak, Paul Goodman

97

PREFACE

This volume addresses itself to some particular writings and to a general theme. Each of the three chapters might stand by itself, for each discusses some small body of critical works and some issues that deserve separate attention. But I think of the issues and works as subsisting within a familiar and very recognizable dilemma that is fundamental to the spiritual history of the West, fundamental perhaps to human experience. And I hope that my more specific subjects will aid in elucidating this dilemma and be further illuminated by it.

The dilemma is that of making a choice or effecting a reconciliation between two imperatives. On the one side is the command and invitation to receive gratefully the rich gifts existence offers us, among them simple feelings as they spring up fresh and uncoerced. On the other is the command, and strangely the appeal, to respond that we encounter in whatever is "hard," willed, austere, in the innumerable disciplines that resist our immediate feelings and appetites. Here we find the stark victories of asceticism over sensuousness, the mundane dignities of exact and difficult workmanship, the endurance of pain, the complex restraints of civilization, and most encompassingly the ceaseless pressures of conscience. In one of its obvious formulations the polarity is between impulse and form, but that does not quite serve. Feelings, as the Vanderbilt critics will demonstrate, may have their own tastes for graceful forms and an ordered life, while the moral will may restlessly set about breaking up comfortable and charming forms as it pursues its sterner objects. Nor can we distinguish between the two imperatives by allying one of them with self-assertion and the other with humility. While the urge to celebration can suggest the way of expressive personalism, it also may imply a self-effacing humility in the presence of life's free and lavish goods, exterior and inward. The command to austerity and discipline can point to a breaking of the self to some larger pattern, or to the attaining of a strong confident personal identity. Among the most subtle and paradoxical resistances the will puts up to appetite is the censure the religious conscience delivers against the very fact of self-conquest, when self-conquest has become moral pride and a state of arrogant aloofness from the gifts that lie around and within us.

A major strategy of civilization, of course, is to negotiate the two categories of experience into fruitful, if precarious, alliances: to bend and twist the world's immediate goods into more elaborate ones, to enlist the disciplines of art for the refinement of feeling, to put morality at the service of love. A task of literature has been to contemplate that strategy in its detail. This book examines a small portion of literature, and in its final form represents, as I have indicated, an intersection of several interests on my part: in the particular works discussed, in a number of issues on which these writings bear, and in the unifying theme. If my ambition had been to do a large cultural history, I could not begin to justify the omissions or the arrangement of choices. But in some specific ways my selections are useful for perceiving the greater dilemma as I have defined it, besides offering their special topics.

For an exact philosophical investigation into the uses of "nature" as a norm for moral and social standards, Thomas Carlyle and George Fitzhugh would scarcely do. But precisely because they look naively rather than with philosophical clarity upon the face of nature, they can show us something about the manner in which nature presents itself to the imagination. I enjoyed trying to bring to some order in a short space my reactions to the positive, vivid, unsystematic vision of Carlyle, an essayist and historian whose works were once part of the intellectual equipment of generations of readers. In particular, I am intrigued to think that my own father, a student just after the turn of the century, was drawn strongly to Carlyle.

Allen Tate, John Crowe Ransom, and Paul Elmer More each have gained an important place in twentieth-century literary criticism; together they raise basic questions about the part that explicit moral ideas and the moral will should have in life and literature. The answers that Tate and Ransom give are in nice contrast to that offered by More. Differences between the school of criticism for which Tate and Ransom have spoken and the school More espoused make up an interesting incident in American literary history.

My final chapter is a look at three authors who help us to think about the moral and spiritual significance of our having transformed our "natural" earth and our primitive selves into an "artificial" civilization. Hannah Arendt brings to the definition of nature and of the fabricated world, and of their situation within the human story, a massive knowledge of mind and culture in the West from classical times. Her definitions provide basic terms for examining the differing and complementary judgments that Theodore Roszak and Paul Goodman, both of them independent and imaginative contributors to modern American cultural radicalism, make of the artificial.

A critical explication of the sort I pursue has to balance its devices, reporting objectively the detail of the literary materials it investigates while it rearranges arguments, replaces emphases, and draws out implications in accordance with a scheme of its own. I have taken numerous liberties. Some of them are matters of omission: I do not talk about Tate and Ransom in their important capacity of poets, or go into Hannah Arendt's studies of totalitarianism. Sometimes I take from a portion of an author's work something other than its logic. In Carlyle's writing, tone and color dominate over precise argumentation, and my centering on image and suggestion can fairly easily justify itself. But a philosopher could be severe with me for treating of Paul Elmer More's Platonism not primarily as a logical system but as a way of sensing the contraries and strains within us and the world, and therefore of apprehending existence as energetic and the moral life as tense. Looking at a philosophical system in this manner is of course a questionable enterprise. Even if I am granted my emphasis on the experiential component of More's philosophy, it may seem odd that I have concentrated on the elements within his Platonism favoring relentless moral activity rather than on the Platonic longing for the stillness and peace where the Forms dwell. In defense I can only plead what I believe is my faithfulness to the character of More's Platonism, and hope that my selectivity there, as in the rest of the book, will be recognized and tolerated.

Besides putting the materials into a special thematic scheme, I conduct many particular arguments with the authors. Yet I often choose to let the explication proceed without comment. I am especially conscious of letting go with hardly a quarrel the elegant cultural conservatisms examined in the middle chapter—the Old South of the Agrarians, and More's insistence on formality in literature—even when I am at odds with them. My silences are determined in part by the economy of my task, which requires me to get quickly from the conservative views themselves to the more general moral and aesthetic questions they touch on. The theme that informs the whole volume seeks no resolution there. Whether a self-conscious morality and a taste for rigorousness and precision can avoid spiritual pride; how discipline and feeling may enhance rather than destroy each other: these are old and possibly intractable questions. But the materials that are the subjects of these essays add something to our perception of the two imperatives and give us some sense of a universe that can accommodate both.

TRW
Washington, D.C.
November 1975

I

THE DEVICES OF NATURE
GEORGE FITZHUGH AND THOMAS CARLYLE

The appeal to Nature as the norm of right conduct and feeling is as powerful as the term "nature" is elusive. The logical problems are obvious. If nature is synonymous with all of reality, how can we speak of some states as being "unnatural" and wrong? If nature is opposed by other actual things and forces, what remains of nature's inclusiveness and commanding power? Yet philosophers and moralists along with the rest of mankind will continue, probably with strong intuitive cause, to identify harmoniousness and health with existence at its hidden depth, with some simple "natural" grain in the texture of life. The idea of nature grasps our imaginations the more strongly when, instead of suggesting only the natural laws of traditional philosophy, it calls up images of concrete physical things, of fields and flocks and the swift blood in us. And because "nature" means all this—moral rightness compounded with organic vigor and human instinct —it is a dangerous as well as an enticing concept. It can be made to ratify the surrender to all sorts of easy emotions and plausible social arrangements that seem as "natural" as the beat of the pulse—war, racism, revenge—when our actual need is to resist them.

thought as it occurs to him, has a winning flavor of eagerness and geniality.

Fitzhugh's essays offer us more than this, however. Strength of mind, perhaps reinforced by a naiveté that does not know how to shape and pare a thesis, has produced a shaggy, suggestive discourse, a good beginning for broad speculation about the character of society. Fitzhugh presumably is not attempting an exact essay in philosophy, and we need not hold him to precise account for the philosophical indiscretions that may result from the employment of "nature" as a norm. The problem that Fitzhugh most likely unknowingly sets for himself and us is a valid and honorable one. He understands society to be the unfolding of wants and feelings, and wishes the social life to be a direct, "natural" fulfillment of them at their best. Here we have a limited and workable meaning for "nature": the word can designate that part of us which is emotional, closer to impulse than to elaborate deliberation and contrivance. But Fitzhugh knows, and has to insist for the sake of his slaveholding South, that the social project is a matter of incessant bringing to order and purpose. How shall the two needs, for "nature" and for willed control, get reconciled? Fitzhugh cannot tell us to our satisfaction, since he seems unaware of the tensions his argument encompasses. Believing, like others who opposed libertarian democracy, that the social state rather than a state of unconnectedness is our natural condition, he simply presumes that slavery is a fact of nature-as-society. Therefore, he makes out slavery to be, in effect, instinctive and "natural." But in the course of his thought he leads us into the dynamics of the living community, which acts and builds by restraining and wins a measure of what it believes to be civilized freedom (Fitzhugh might be uncomfortable with the word) by assuming to itself the most intricate compulsions.

Fitzhugh's society springs straight and green from the ground of nature. In addition to possessing a powerful drive to self-interest, people are naturally gregarious, he insists. He finds here a phenomenon of organic nature, or that part of organic nature that is cooperative rather than competitive, identifying the social instinct among human beings with that among the more sociable of the lower creatures. Gregariousness, though, is strongest in mankind: it is a benevolence that the individual holds toward those nearest him, then toward far strangers, and toward the whole of outer nature. "A parched field distresses him, and he rejoices as he sees the groves, and the gardens, and the plains flourishing, and blooming, and smiling about him." [1]

Society is to be a growth of nature, and not only the nature of the philosophers, the perfect ultimate or interior form of things, but a nature that is vital, organic, immediate. And if we are to draw our health from that natural world, then we must allow nothing artificial to intrude into its working. Fitzhugh holds the attempt to shape governments on philosophical principles to be more presumptuous than would be the effort to make a tree, which is far less complex

1. George Fitzhugh, *Cannibals All! or Slaves Without Masters*, edited by C. Vann Woodward (Cambridge, Massachusetts: Harvard University Press, The Belknap Press, 1960), p. 36.

than a society. Laws, institutions, governments, societies, trees—all of them grow, and mankind must content itself with careful trimming and cultivation of them. After society has worked for a sufficient time, Fitzhugh declares, people may by observation discover its laws: the English constitution and common law were such discoveries. "Those institutions were the growth and accretions of many ages, not the work of legislating philosophers." [2] Fitzhugh would shun the ways of philosophy, preferring common sense and, above all, Christianity, which "proposes to lead us through the trials and intricacies of life, not by the mere cool calculations of the head, but by the unerring instincts of a pure and regenerate heart." [3]

A society that comes into being by natural growth, a humanity that rejects the artificial devices of the intellect and submits to the promptings of instinct—to get from this to Southern slavery, with its elaborate and deliberate projects on the part of the slaveholder and its denial of freedom and spontaneity to the slave, appears to require a chasmic leap. Since *Sociology for the South* and *Cannibals All!* make the leap by something closer to unconscious presumptions than to conscious logic, we must supply the implicit argument.

In its practical character, slavery by Fitzhugh's description is the means whereby the latent com-

2. George Fitzhugh, *Sociology for the South, or the Failure of Free Society* (New York: Burt Franklin, 1965), pp. 175–76.
3. *Sociology for the South*, pp. 10–11, 118–19; *Cannibals All!*, p. 37.

munity is made active, the affections and the self-interest of the individual so directed that they render men truly social. Fitzhugh's argument is in part a common contention of his era: slavery identifies labor with capital and therefore makes the owner as much concerned for the welfare of labor as the Northern capitalist is solicitous of his abstract and inanimate possessions.[4] But Fitzhugh's human being is a creature more of instinct and passion than of rational strategy, and even self-interest comes out to be something beyond economic calculation. Fitzhugh will argue, to be sure, that the size of the slave owner's investment in his workers guarantees his good care of them; but at one point in *Sociology for the South* the "selfishness of man's nature," which operates to the advantage of the slave, becomes an affectionate sense of possession that binds an owner even to beings he possesses but cannot exploit. We are given a picture of a plantation that is not so much an economic unit as a comfortable family in which the able work and the helpless are sheltered. To this situation Fitzhugh does not hesitate to apply the term "community of property"; and property, he observes, is "a mere creature of law and society," for which the wealthy owe a return to the public that gives them their possessions.[5]

Is slavery, then, no more than a system of adjustments by which instincts are led gently to social ends? No, it is also a system of unceasing force. Force, the constant application of government and will to people without their consent, is the need; and

4. *Cannibals All!*, pp. 28, 30–31, 34.
5. *Sociology for the South*, pp. 27, 45–48, 105–7.

Fitzhugh criticizes strictly construed constitutions because they limit the act of government. He does suggest that force by its ubiquitousness can become second nature to its subjects: the citizen "fulfills *con amore*, his round of social, political, and domestic duties, and never dreams that the Law, with its fines and jails, penitentiaries and halters, or Public Opinion, with its ostracism, its mobs, and its tar and feathers, help[s] to keep him revolving in his orbit." [6] But these habits, as this passage describes them, are impressed upon the citizen, not drawn out of his instinctual self.

Fitzhugh leads us even further from the nature on which he had thought to found the human enterprise. In the end, Fitzhugh's social man takes to himself all the skill and device that belong to an advanced economy. Fitzhugh wanted such an economy for the South; his argument for manufacturing is in effect a demand for trained and civilized intelligence.

Commerce between a manufacturing and an agricultural region, Fitzhugh proposes, amounts to the exploitation of the agricultural. The reason, or part of it, is that manufacture because of its superiority in skill expends less labor than farming must undergo in exchange; industry can, in essence, command the labor of agriculture. And the intelligence that manufacturing collects to itself and awakens through its mechanical arts and labor is an enrichment to the civilization in which it operates, while a landed economy must sink into cultural somnolence.[7]

6. *Cannibals All!*, pp. 243–44, 249.
7. *Sociology for the South*, pp. 14–15, 149–60, 172–74.

The solution for Fitzhugh is the achievement of regional autonomy: the abandonment of free trade in economics and imitation in culture. In this call to regionalism, Fitzhugh at once takes us to the furthest point of a willed and contrived civilization and yet returns us to nature. The exclusion of foreign manufacture, it appears, will summon forth the inventive resources: "Man's necessities civilize him, or rather the labor, invention and ingenuity needed to supply them"; "invention alone begets civilization."[8] But what of instinct is left to this civilization that labor and intelligence have wrought into being? The answer lies in metaphor, the metaphor of organism and growth. Necessities and circumstance translate themselves implicitly into the earth from which the regional civilization springs; the response to them becomes not so much contrivance as organic process. Protesting against cultural centralization, the fiat of Paris, Fitzhugh can depict regional culture in just this fashion; it must develop according to its internal need and logic, preserving its dialect, for example, from the stiff rules of grammar. "Nature is always grammatical, and language, the child of nature, would continue so but for the grammarians, who, with their Procrustean rules, disturb its proportions, destroy its variety and adaptation, and retard its growth."[9]

Actually, Fitzhugh's society is an extended metaphor, born of an elaborated sensibility rather than of rigorous observation or of anything like social science as we would now conceive of it. This is not

8. Ibid., pp. 19–20.
9. *Cannibals All!*, pp. 59–60.

a weakness. Fitzhugh takes us to the paradoxical center of our own feelings toward society; by metaphor he catches our contradictory intuitions about the impulsive living humanity and the imposed conditions that together we expect of civilized existence. But there *Sociology for the South* and *Cannibals All!* stop, because Fitzhugh has not defined the tension, or explored minutely the actual workings of an accomplished civilization that he has chosen to describe fundamentally as a function of nature and force. The great fact he has overlooked is one that he comes very close to identifying when he talks of regional dialect with its nicely shaded adaptations to the needs and thoughts of the community, or when he pictures the civilized inventive intelligence, itself trained up by the presence of invention.

This fact that Fitzhugh cannot quite fix upon might best go by the word "artificiality," if that term can cover the innumerable choices and the pervasive delicate pressures coming from the human environment and its artifacts, through which the inanimate things of civilization come into being and each of its inhabitants receives or purposefully acquires a specific character and personality. (Hannah Arendt, we shall see, uses "artifice" in a much more precise way, to mean mostly the durable physical objects, made by human hands, that serve as a foundation for the political community.) Artificiality as I am defining it cannot be equated with nature, if nature is understood to be emotion, instinct, and the human participation in organic life; nor can artificiality be confused with raw force. Measured against artificiality, Fitzhugh's apparent identification of nature with force takes on a certain logic, for the force that you apply to other human beings expresses your "natural" emotion and wish rather than contradicting them; the force that you submit to does not require from you a chosen, subtle, and self-disciplined resistance to your impulsive nature.

At one eloquent moment, when Fitzhugh is defending his discursive, disordered method of argument, he reveals a taste that would militate against the condition I have termed "artificiality": "We admire not the pellucid rivulet, that murmurs and meanders, in cramped and artificial current, through the park and gardens of the nobleman; but we do admire the flooded and swollen Mississippi," bearing the diverse things swept from its shores. "The Exhaustive, not the Artistic, is what we would aspire to." [10] The passage could serve as an image not only for Fitzhugh's argumentation but for the society he describes, dense with nature, custom, and tradition, swift with forceful unreflective act. But that description will not adequately serve even for the actual South he has claimed to represent.

The bringing to light of the artificial things that made up antebellum slavery—the precise forms of its disciplines, the interplay of economics and social institutions, the living flavor of slave-quarter culture, and the culturally grounded consciousness of the individual slave—is what a good deal of recent scholarship on the era of Southern slavery is about. Once social man is seen in this way, as a creature in whom biological "nature" has been refracted through an

10. Ibid., p. 239.

25

artificial culture, while force is only the crudest of
the influences that culture wields, he eludes the
terms Fitzhugh has set for discussing him; and slavery stands condemned for being the least civilized,
the least subtle and artificial institution of culture
the South could have held to. Surely Fitzhugh in life
knew much of the Southern artifice. His two essays
halt short of concretely analyzing his surroundings:
they remain brilliantly provocative sketchings of the
primary elements, of the natural inclination and imposed force, that go into a civilized life, with little
exact thought about the civilized artificiality that is
more elaborately deliberate than nature, more tactful
than force.

✻   ✻   ✻   ✻

Fitzhugh would have welcomed being com-
pared to Thomas Carlyle, whom he happily quotes.
There is more similarity between the two than their
defense of slavery and social coercion. Carlyle, like
Fitzhugh, describes the oneness of man with nature,
and the collective oneness of mankind; and he sets
humanity on another richly contradictory enterprise
compounded of intuitive submission and radical acts
of the creative will.

Carlyle does not offer a coherent logical system;
he is to be sought in the abundance of imagery and
abrupt phrasing. What we find are not ideas precisely but a number of controlling tastes—informed,
to be sure, by a Carlylean version of Romanticism on

some German model. The vocabulary is all color and shape and action—great craggy bulks of things emerge, and then will come a moment of fine line and cool light. It is preeminently a vigorous vocabulary, in its exaltation of the harder virtues, its concept of a nature that is force, the thick hulking forms it flings out.

The first impression is of massive weight—of force in its profusions rather than its economies. Here, in *Heroes and Hero-Worship* (1840), is the Iceland of the Norse: "burst up, the geologists say, by fire from the bottom of the sea; a wild land of barrenness and lava; . . . with its snow jokuls, roaring geysers, sulphur-pools and horrid volcanic chasms, like the waste chaotic battle-field of Frost and Fire." Carlyle praises the Norse for "their robust simplicity; their veracity, directness of conception. Thor 'draws down his brows' in a veritable Norse rage; 'grasps his hammer till the *knuckles grow white.*' " [11] It is the typical mode of the Carlylean sensibility, bearing importantly upon the themes that most concern us here. For it perceives a universe fleshed, various, and substantial, fleshed like those other great solid things—history, institution, land— with which some of our authors give body to existence.

Another kind of imagery also flecks the writings. Describing, in "Characteristics" (1831), the healthy spontaneity of nature before it has been invaded by inquiry, Carlyle recalls "seasons of a light, aerial

11. "On Heroes, Hero-Worship, and the Heroic in History," *The Complete Works of Thomas Carlyle,* 10 vols. (New York, The Kelmscott Society, c. 1912), X: 249, 267.

translucency and elasticity and perfect freedom," and imagines a life that might be "a pure, perpetual, unregarded music; a beam of perfect white light, rendering all things visible, but itself unseen, even because it was of that perfect whiteness, and no irregular obstruction had yet broken it into colors." [12] Here the light and purity come of a primal condition; in "The Life of Heyne" (1828), they belong to states of sophistication: "philosophic order, . . . classical adjustment, clearness, polish." [13] Such points of light and clarity become themselves variegations within the heavy, lavish texture of existence as Carlyle pictures it.

An ultimate measure for Carlyle is nature or some like reality. The concept is again elusive, threatening to expand into tautology or contract beyond usefulness. One of the nearest conceptual equivalents is Force: Professor Teufelsdröckh of *Sartor Resartus* (1831) announces of a smithy fire glowing across a moor that it was " 'kindled at the Sun; is fed by air that circulates from before Noah's Deluge, from beyond the Dogstar; therein, with Iron Force, and Coal Force, and the far stranger Force of Man, are cunning affinities and battles and victories of Force brought about.' " [14] At another moment the reality will appear as a powerful event, such as the democracy that swept aside institutions become useless; or reality will be the laws of matter, which permit no violation, laws that workers vindicate them-

12. "Characteristics," in *Complete Works*, III: 345.
13. "The Life of Heyne," in *Complete Works*, III: 348–49.
14. "Sartor Resartus," in *Complete Works*, X: 54.

selves by obeying. *Sartor Resartus*, as splendid in image and style as it is indefinite in logic, relates the Clothes-Philosophy of Professor Teufelsdröckh, a vision of a cosmic reality that dresses itself in its phenomenal vestments as people express themselves in cloth and leather. A reality that is also active, compelling force, Carlyle's nature demands obedience by moral obligation, and exacts obedience with the irresistible stubbornness of reality itself. "All that is *right*," proclaims *Heroes and Hero-Worship*, "includes itself in this of co-operating with the real Tendency of the World: you succeed by this (the World's Tendency will succeed), you are good, and in the right course there." [15]

Carlyle's nature is Fact; it demands of us total submission—except that since it is encompassing fact, the very concept of rebellion against it would seem to be meaningless. Therefore, we need some principle of differentiation, some way for the moral will to exercise positive choice at the same time that it is bound to the reality it must morally serve. Once more, we get from Carlyle a fleeting, rhetorical solution rather than a logical one. Somewhere at the margin of the universe exists such a thing as falsehood, or non-fact, or at least an ability to trifle; people are free to be unserious about the Fact that they encounter and belong to. And to trifle, to be light-headed and superficial, is for Carlyle a sin, as a hard sincerity about nature and fact is virtue. In *Heroes and Hero-Worship* he writes of Mohammed, "The great Mystery of Existence . . . glared in upon

15. "Heroes and Hero-Worship," in *Complete Works*, X: 294.

him, with its terrors, with its splendors; no hearsays could hide that unspeakable fact, 'Here am I!' Such *sincerity* . . . has in very truth something of divine." [16] To stand stripped and awestruck before reality, to perceive it—naively and roughly, perhaps, for these are attributes of sincerity: this is nearly the essence of virtue.

Here we spoke of virtue at its most strenuous. In "Characteristics" Carlyle describes a gentler unity with nature—a state of unconsciousness, in which no element of life has yet achieved, in malaise, an awareness of its separate self and begun announcing its independent existence. It is the condition we possessed at times in our early life, when we did not know of our limbs—"we only lifted, hurled and leapt; through eye and ear, and all avenues of sense, came clear unimpeded tidings from without, and from within issued clear victorious force"; and we were in harmony with all around us. Such is also, Carlyle argues, the state of social health: society unconscious of its structure, its workings all in accord with one another.[17] Do we have here a time of Edenic innocence? Perhaps, but the spontaneity Carlyle is defining can appear outside the Garden of Eden. The societies he finds to have been healthy possessed their uncontrived fluency in feeling and act in the midst of non-Edenic struggles and labors; and Carlyle discovers a similar quality in the process of great and complex artistic work. Shakespeare's art, he writes in *Heroes and Hero-Worship*, "is not Artifice;

16. Ibid., p. 285.
17. "Characteristics," in *Complete Works*, III: 344–48, 355–58.

the noblest worth of it is not there by plan or pre-contrivance. . . . Such a man's works, whatsoever he with utmost conscious exertion and forethought shall accomplish, grow up withal *un*consciously, from the unknown deeps in him." [18] The strain in temper between light youthful harmony and a burning prophetic earnestness provides an interesting complication within the state of virtue—the sort of complication, unrecognized apparently by the author, that the reader will occasionally fall upon in Carlyle's writings.

One point of morality is sure: man is justified by his labor. In work, the laborer puts himself into submission to the forces of reality; he makes himself their instrument, and almost prophetlike, he sees them. Work is revelation. A member of Parliament can reason in a void with no penalty, Carlyle writes in "Corn-Law Rhymes" (1832); "but the sooty Brazier, who discovered that brass was green-cheese, has to act on his discovery; finds therefore, that, singular as it may seem, brass cannot be masticated for dinner, green-cheese will not beat into fire-proof dishes." [19] The good worker finds the natural forms of things, works along the true lines of force. Admiring Voltaire, Carlyle nonetheless says of him in an essay of 1829 that his objects lie not "in pictorial, not always in scientific grouping; but rather in commodious rows. . . . We might say," Carlyle complains, that "there is not the deep natural symmetry of a forest oak, but the simple artificial symmetry of

18. "Heroes and Hero-Worship," in *Complete Works,* X: 335.
19. "Corn-Law Rhymes," in *Complete Works,* IV: 127.

on the political left and the political right—the myth of collectivity.

Carlyle talks of societies as though they are single, collective things. While that conception of countries and peoples is common, Carlyle gives it his own poetic stamp. His societies are as dark and massy as the nature out of which they come through slow centuries and sudden leadership; and so, in the grand metaphor of soil and organism, he says of Scots literature in "Burns" (1828) that it grows no longer "in water but in mould, and with the true racy virtues of the soil and climate."[25] Societies are also instinctive and quick with the forces of nature. Carlyle's heroes unify their societies by flashes of clear insight into the truths their people have dimly perceived, and their words kindle together the separate minds of their followers into a flame of collective idea. Carlyle's societies appear to be projections out of some primitive sense, yet they may gain expression in civilized thought and literature. Carlyle pictures collective states that seem to dissolve the particularities composing them: "Every Society . . . is the embodiment . . . of an Idea: all its tendencies of endeavor, specialities of custom, its laws, politics and whole procedure . . . are prescribed by an Idea, and flow naturally from it, as movements from the living source of motion."[26] But a passage like this, from "Boswell's Life of Johnson" (1832): "Nothing dies, nothing can die. No idlest word thou speakest but is a seed cast into Time, and grows through

25. "Burns," in *Complete Works*, III: 286.
26. "Characteristics," in *Complete Works*, III: 356.

all Eternity!" [27]—such a passage gives a historical process that does not completely impose itself upon the individual but to the contrary is spun together of separate acts.

We may put up with some of the more grating elements in Carlyle's social philosophy. He exalts the hero, who has a commission from nature itself to rule over the people among whom he is placed; Carlyle even finds a dictator or two who fills the hero's place. But aside from these, Carlyle's heroes need not offend us: many of them turn out to be prophets, poets, and others of similar role—Mohammed, Dante, Shakespeare, Luther, even so unferocious a person as Robert Burns. Besides, the Carlylean hero really is interesting not so much for his own dominating presence as for the virtuous things Carlyle associates with him: the earnest, naked reception of nature's fact and command; the noble loyalties the great man elicits from the people about him. Nor is there point in dwelling on Carlyle's defense of slavery, which is no longer susceptible of being awakened into intellectual argument. Again, the subject itself is interesting mostly for being a vehicle for some broader notions Carlyle offers of society and the unbreakable bonds among its members. We cannot conceivably make Carlyle out to be a reactionary. He admires a sturdy conservatism for its weight and toughness, in which it partakes of the Carlylean morality and style: "And greatly do I respect the solid character,—a blockhead, thou wilt say; yes, but a well-conditioned blockhead, and the best-con-

27. "Boswell's Life of Johnson," in *Complete Works*, III: 423.

ditioned,—who esteems all 'Customs once solemnly acknowledged' to be ultimate, divine, and the rule for a man to walk by, nothing doubting, not inquiring farther." [28] But Carlyle, as he reveals in *The French Revolution* (1837), has a great sense of historical change, which he understands to be the work of casting off forms gone corrupt and getting back to the heart of nature. At any rate, he presumes that in democracy, which he does not much like in its liberal egalitarian character, nature is getting at something important and inevitable; its full meaning has yet to effect itself.

The problem that Carlyle's myth of collectivity raises is a variant of the larger ambiguity. Since his societies and times arise with a natural spontaneity and take the forms that go easily about their vital selves, the role of the constructive will is uncertain, though at moments Carlyle appears to put the will at the center of the social process. As in the pages of Fitzhugh, we lose sight of the civilized artificiality, the fragile creations that are triumphs precisely in their fragility and the care with which they are willed and sustained. Voltaire's writings, we have heard Carlyle say, have "not the deep natural symmetry of a forest oak, but the simple artificial symmetry of a parlor chandelier." But are parlor chandeliers not among the kinds of things whereby a culture affirms its ingenuity and its urge to give shape to things?

28. "Past and Present," in *Complete Works*, VIII: 158–59.

In denying to history its contrivances, moreover, we take from it the variation in detail that the full historical sensibility looks for. An age becomes merely the expression of a single guiding spirit; its texture lacks the individual, quirky facts that come of the separate intelligences composing it. Yet it is in the feeling for texture and substance that Carlyle has so much to offer.

Carlyle's conception of social oneness, however, goes beyond all this, and at its best relies on the same intuition as that from which Fitzhugh argues, the conviction that people belong to one another. Gurth, thrall of Cedric the Saxon, tending Cedric's pigs, with a brass collar around his neck, had the sky above, the air and life around him, "and in him at least the certainty of supper and social lodging when he came home." He "had the inexpressible satisfaction of feeling himself related indissolubly, though in a rude brass-collar way, to his fellow-mortals in this Earth. He had superiors, inferiors, equals." Now Gurth is emancipated; but has he been given the " 'Liberty to die by starvation' "? Carlyle can be content that the "brass-collar method" of connecting people has disappeared: "Huge Democracy, walking the streets everywhere in its Sack Coat, has asserted so much; irrevocably, brooking no reply!" But the individual needs still to be connected with the rest of mankind; we have to have "far nobler and cunninger methods" than that of the brass collar for binding him. He is "to have a scope *as* wide as his faculties now are." Send him forth free and trusted, and he will come back to you "with rich earnings at night!" [29]

Carlyle's strength is in robustness of vocabulary and vision, and there lie his limits. He tends toward heavy, rank images, interspersed with lighter ones; his liking for thick substantiality accompanies a concept of densely connected communities that for all its failings is an ingratiating and honorable contribution to the war against liberal atomism. The same vocabulary gives its tone to the morality and asceticism that Carlyle preaches. He describes moral states that are essentially muscular: large acts of renunciation, mammoth single-minded endeavors, earnest silence. A cooler asceticism—the quest for precision, the endurance of complexity, the distortion of impulse to the detail and intricacy of some highly civilized task—is seldom touched, although Carlyle gives hints of it. Carlyle will admire the industrial age for its great massive work: "The grim inarticulate veracity of the English People, unable to speak its meaning in words, has turned itself silently on things," and nature has answered: " 'Mountains, old as the Creation, I have permitted to be bored through. . . . Your huge fleets, steamships, do sail the sea." [30] Carlyle's phrases are right for an industrialism of steam and iron, its labors expressive of coarse power; a later technology, proceeding by

29. Ibid., pp. 205, 241.
30. Ibid., p. 164.

closer and more delicate disciplines and taking to itself the spare lines and surfaces of modern architecture, would have eluded the Carlylean vocabulary. But what Carlyle has given us is a compelling morality of submission and purpose.

❊   ❊   ❊   ❊

Carlyle's rhetoric cannot resolve the conflicts within a morality that commands obedience to fact. The paradox is not his alone. It belongs to the state of reverence itself, which demands purposeful moral act within a cosmos that we also know to be plenteous and full and everlasting, and sustains the experience of moral tension upon an experience of assurance and peace. And it is within experience rather than logic that Carlyle and Fitzhugh place themselves—Fitzhugh in his simple intuition of community, Carlyle in the sternness and density of the natural and social existence his words evoke, both writers in their feeling for the richness and potency of the universe on which human life in its limitation can draw.

II

THE DIVIDED CONSCIOUSNESS
ALLEN TATE, JOHN CROWE RANSOM,
PAUL ELMER MORE

In two published essays given in substance as talks in 1951, Allen Tate illustrates through Dante and Edgar Allan Poe a distinction between the "symbolic" and the "angelic" imagination. By the angelic imagination Tate means the human effort to achieve the knowledge that is possible only for angels, the direct knowledge of essences; the symbolic imagination keeps within the limits finite man must observe and contents itself with indirectly approaching the ultimate things through the images provided in the natural world. The symbolic imagination was the mode of pre-Reformation Christianity, the mode of Dante; the angelic imagination made its appearance in more modern times. It is represented, if I am correct about Tate's meaning, in recent science and the other intellectual assaults that man now makes upon the cosmos; and Tate presents Poe as having brilliant insight into its character and its disintegration of the personality. It is recognizable in the vision, appearing throughout Poe's writings, of a universe in which the stable material substance is dissolved and remade wholly into a thing of intellect or dream; it is to be found in the love between Poe's characters, a love that attempts to bypass the natural order and the carnal connection and to seize directly upon the essence of the beloved. Poe's lovers pursue a "mutual destruction of soul." [1]

The essays read like a theological rendering of positions that Tate had earlier sustained in the company of some remarkable cultural and literary critics. In brief and with variations, it was an insistence upon concreteness, even materiality of a sort, in experience, and it sought to define facts that have a high order of concreteness to them. The land as a tangible, delimiting, and satisfying alternative to the abstractions of the social reformers and the ideologues; the poetic metaphor that can transform rational statements, taking them into its earthy substance; the old Christianity in the vividness it had possessed before modernism bleached it out, the Christianity that fixed not on big general ideas but on things like history and incident, with a rough grain of fact to them.

This substantiality is the context, so it was argued, for wholeness and for a plain and bountiful health. The condition that Tate and his fellow critics were defining, however, is delicate and of a fine tension. Actually, we are dealing not with one condition but with a number of associations between substantial experience and forms that are inherent in experience, or shelter it, or complete and contradict it.

I'll Take My Stand, a book of essays commending the South and its agrarian tradition, was published in 1930. All of the essayists were Southern, and most of them had an association with Vanderbilt

1. Allen Tate, "The Angelic Imagination," in *Collected Essays* (Denver: Alan Swallow, 1959), p. 435.

University; during the nineteen twenties some had belonged to a circle of poets centered in Nashville and going by the name of the Fugitives. The twelve, some of whom would later move to other persuasions, came to be known as the Agrarians. Each of the pieces sustains an admirable intelligence, and the book is as pleasant and enticing an argument as its cause could have. On the whole the work avoids romanticism about a great planter civilization, instead contenting itself with describing in excellent conversational prose a few solid, healthy, and elegant attributes that a reasonably successful society can be believed to possess.

That is the approximate tone in the first of the twelve essays, John Crowe Ransom's "Reconstructed but Unregenerate." The South, Ransom argues, reenacted the wisdom of landed England, which was the wisdom to get over the pioneering phase as quickly as possible. The pioneer who intends to remain one has chosen to make war on nature and is, in effect, an industrialist and progressive. The better course is to test the land, see what it offers and what it will not permit, and settle with it on some comfortable working terms. So accepted, as the South accepted it, treated humbly and with leisurely, kindly attention, the land will offer continuing delight. The other essays consider the modest triumphs of living that their authors think they perceive in the traditional South, or define some ill of modernity and industrialism.

The arts, claims Donald Davidson in "A Mirror for Artists," are unavailable to an industrial civilization, for they cannot be bought; they flourish only if the environment itself is consonant with them, and a good environment for them is agrarian. Frank Lawrence Owsley's "The Irrepressible Conflict" is a contribution to the historiographical controversy over the Civil War, which Owsley describes as a clash between an agrarian and an industrial society. John Gould Fletcher's "Education, Past and Present" finds the educational system of the Old South to offer a training in character and general excellence that is not to be found in the school systems of modern America. "A Critique of the Philosophy of Progress" is an examination by a social scientist, Lyle H. Lanier, of the contradictions between human nature and the schemes and expectations of modern progressives. Tate's "Remarks on the Southern Religion" elects for the fullness and factuality of old-time Southern Christianity in opposition to religious modernism.

In "Whither Southern Economy?" Herman Clarence Nixon argues vigorously for the superiority of the Southern agricultural economy to an unbalanced industrialism. Andrew Nelson Lytle in "The Hind Tit" describes the robust and independent life of a Southern farm family and traces its decline as it ensnares itself in modern technology. Robert Penn Warren comments on the race problem in "The Briar Patch." If Warren's call for a largely separate development and elaboration of the black community under conditions of justice does not go very far toward a twentieth-century liberalism, he nonetheless writes with seriousness and humanity. The fictional hero in John Donald Wade's "The Life and Death of Cousin Lucius" is both a gentleman and a

pragmatist, progressive enough to work for an en-
lightened agriculture in his neighborhood, traditional enough to shrink from commercialism. Henry
Blue Kline's "William Remington: A Study in In-
dividualism" sets its character on an exploration of
himself and a search for a satisfactory environment
that bring him to the South, where a person of
autonomy and taste can draw nourishment. Stark
Young's "Not in Memoriam, but in Defense" considers the Southern mind at its best, and the meaning
of good manners.

Deliberately or not, the Agrarians had hit on a
good strategy. It is also an intellectually appropriate
strategy for the moral and aesthetic doctrine of tangible experience for which some of their number would
contend. With their easy manner of description and
their curiosity about the detail of Southern life, the
authors have an air of searching out the concrete
situation. Here is an imperfect society that once
existed and still exists in fragments despite the New
South, they seem to say; its achievements were not
visibly great, and it produced no *Summa* through
which to reveal its mind. We believe that its special
homely virtues will recommend themselves to you.
But we want you to know them as facts should be
known, by encounter rather than by abstraction; and
so we have put exposition above philosophy.

The agrarian society that the authors depict
looks like the solid and limiting reality Tate will
commend in his later essays on the symbolic and the
angelic imagination. The land is, of course, the dominating presence; but other elements, awakened in
response to the land or subsisting on their own, of-

fer themselves: community, tradition, and a good stock of habits and manners. These are to persuade us by being available, almost, to the sense of touch, and it is by the same means and not by logic, so we may decide, that they commanded the peoples who lived under them.

The liberal case against the essays is clear enough, and there would be no object here in debating their authors point by point. The volume deserves to be met, respected, and criticized with reference to its own basic intuitions about society and human need. Our main quarrel might be precisely over one of its most attractive qualities—the preference among its authors for societies in a condition of harmonious wholeness, innocent of the moral and intellectual tautness that they would dismiss as representing moralism, or the war on nature, or the destructive ambition for progress. Davidson, for example, in his strong and persuasive essay attacks what he identifies as the industrialist theory of the arts, that leisure and wealth will purchase them, and responds that art will not thrive unless its environment can integrate itself more directly into the awareness and work of the artist. He speaks for agrarian environments as being able so to sustain the aesthetic experience. The essay takes no account of the benefits that art might draw from rougher contacts with a milieu marked by the jagged and restless shapes of machinery and by the scientific dissolution of the forms our common sense once took for granted: it might draw, as the art of our century has indeed taken, a feeling for radical forms.

Good manners, a branch of conduct that an impatient moralist may too loftily dismiss, receive their attention. To the critics who would favor a blunt sincerity to Southern manners, Stark Young replies in this way: when you say "I'm glad to see you" to someone you don't really want to see at the moment, you are truthfully reporting your feeling about him "by the year"—"you are . . . insincere by the moment but sincere by the year." By such acts, Young says in effect, you confirm the enduring relationships among people that give a good society its texture, instead of the momentary encounters governed by egotism and whim. "Manners are the mask of decency that we employ at need, the currency of fair communication; their flower is a common grace, and their fruit not seldom friendship." [2] There are, Young proposes, "certain things . . . that, according to what I had always been taught, belong to decorum, to our *mores* rather than to our morals," certain matters of good conduct that are governed more by taste than by moral logic.[3] It is not far different from the argument that Tate makes in his essay for the volume when he observes of the correspondence between Thomas Jefferson and John Adams that the New Englander wanted to place morality in a "process of moral reasoning" while his Southern friend would establish morality in "taste." [4]

2. Stark Young, "Not in Memorium, but in Defense," in Twelve Southerners, *I'll Take My Stand: The South and the Agrarian Tradition,* introduction by Louis D. Rubin, Jr., biographical essays by Virginia Rock (New York: Harper and Row, Harper Torchbooks, 1962), pp. 345–46.

3. Ibid., p. 340.

4. Allen Tate, "Remarks on the Southern Religion," in *I'll Take My Stand,* p. 170.

That, again, is the trouble. The sense of manners can make up a morality often more attractive, possibly of deeper grain, and certainly less dangerous to bystanders than is the conscience of a determined moralist. Yet we would want courtesy to be governed by a moral will that can sharpen it on the personal level, and on the social level quicken it into an active and compassionate politics, even at the risk of disintegrating it into a ferocious moralism. This does represent a risky and fragile balance, but it is a desirable one. Warren's contribution shows such a balance, Southern manners informed by a conscience too rare in the South of the 1920s and 1930s. At a time when Southern integration must have seemed out of the question given the attitude of the white majority and its absolute domination of local politics, Warren was determined at least to argue for a more decent and equitable separatism. His sensibility grew with the growth of the civil rights revolution, and he became one of the South's most finely tempered liberals, joining an integrationist persuasion to a full and receptive understanding of the Southern region.

The simplicity of antebellum Southern culture, and the absence within it of clashing forces, got two descriptions from Allen Tate at widely separate moments of his career. Tate's biography of Stonewall Jackson, published in 1928, contains the observation that the Southerner's character, his moral identity, lay in his property, which gave him a public presence. "The idea of the 'inner life', held by the Calvinist people in far-off New England, had no meaning. In the South, the man as he appeared in public was the man: his public appearance was his moral

crete undissected objects on which experience can fully nourish itself; and on the other are rigorous forms, clear intellectual concepts, sharp acts of the will—pressing against experience, at once imperiling and perfecting it. We end with something different from the South of *I'll Take My Stand,* but we have a situation complex, precarious, and very rich.

"Forms and Citizens," an essay included in Ransom's *The World's Body* (1938), gives one sort of relationship. The worth of forms, Ransom says, is that they stand between a person and an object of his emotions and, by halting the immediate rush of appetite, complicate appetite into sensibility. The forms of manners, as they are found in courtship, require the lover to come to his beloved indirectly, contemplate her through careful courting, and in the contemplation know her in her individuality. Religious ritual, again, turns passion into sensibility. And the restraining indirections of poetry are a technique for contemplating objects with attention and respect.

"The Mimetic Principle," printed in the same volume, looks more closely at the role of art in the preservation of loved objects—individuals, Ransom calls them there. Drawing upon a classical definition of art as mimesis or imitation, the essay reasons that the motive for this imitation is love for the original, as the motive for science is exploitation. The scientist wants to put universals into control of particulars. He examines the individual object not for its individuality but for its consistencies with others of its kind, consistencies that can be translated into laws and put to use; and the object is dissolved into abstractions.

The artist intends to preserve the particular, and so he makes an imitation that, being an imitation, cannot possibly be used: an elaborate contemplating of the particularity the original has, the limitless density of line and color that it possesses as an independent being.

The object in its particularity that we discover in *The World's Body* is essentially the tangible, health-giving fact that the Agrarian essays identify with the land, and Tate will later set to nourishing the symbolic imagination. But its bearing on us is differently described. The land of Ransom's Agrarian essay is a dominating force, tolerant of us only if we approach it humbly. The material world Tate recommends in "The Symbolic Imagination: The Mirrors of Dante" is an instructor, a vehicle of truths. Each presides over us in some way. The object we hear of in "Forms and Citizens" and "The Mimetic Principle," on the other hand, is fragile, needing protection against the brutal experiential urges it may first awaken in us, or against the scientific effort to think it into its usable components; it is not safe until the discipline of forms has made our experiencing delicate. And this means that consciousness is divided. The given and durable objects of *I'll Take My Stand*—the soil, and the scarcely less tangible facts of habits and codes—all speak to consciousness in about the same way, so that the responsive awareness the Southerner has of his land is like his awareness of the conversational proprieties and his awareness of right morals; feeling is of a single texture with moral thought. The moral, or more accurately the aesthetic, will that we find in *The World's Body*, to the contrary, must wage a difficult battle against the feelings and turn them from aggressive hunger to loving sensibility. The word "moral" is inserted here quite arbitrarily. Ransom has not taken to the task of the moralists, considering it to be, like the scientists' work, one of quantifying and of reduction to the universals. But I think the word fits the artistic forms in the painstaking care with which they come to the protection of the loved objects.

Although Ransom's two essays divide the consciousness, that is not what they are about; the division is inexplicit. This leaves us with "The Tense of Poetry," in which Ransom does speculate about a clash within us.

Ransom does not, in "Forms and Citizens" and "The Mimetic Principle," define the nature of the objects or individuals he wants art to protect from our lower passions. The argument is so cast as to apply most easily to persons and things having an existence "objectively" apart from us. In "The Tense of Poetry" Ransom discusses a subject that, if not one of his "objects," is nonetheless worthy of an equal solicitude: he discusses our own sensibility, as it had been in its primal condition. This, we might suppose, is precisely the condition of primitive hunger that Ransom has called upon the artist to war against. But in "The Tense of Poetry" he means a sensibility as fresh and innocent as in the Garden of Eden. The essay considers the story of the garden and of the knowledge or rationality that invaded it. The elements of the divided consciousness, then, will be innocent feeling on the one side and scientific or technical reason on the other. Ransom will give to this rationality an honorable part in the making of a higher sensibility, and the essay holds a suggestive ambivalence.

The subject is poetic nostalgia. The source of the nostalgia, Ransom proposes, is our memory of innocence, and of the aggression that reason has committed on innocence. At what time was the aggression? Nostalgia may be "the concrete form of our time-sense. The basis of that sense becomes in this event a biological experience: the outrage performed upon one function of the mind, the aesthetic, by the progress of the other function, the efficient." [8] This appears to set innocence in childhood and science in our maturity; or, since much of *The World's Body* is an attack on the presumptions of science, Ransom could be taken to mean that innocence has belonged to the historical childhood of mankind and knowledge or science to its corrupt adulthood. But we have another possibility, which the indefiniteness of the essay permits. This is to suppose a continuing coexistence of reason and innocence, or fresh sensibility: the reason—invited into action by innocent curiosity—making its incessant cuts into the innocence, even while its new cores of hard knowledge awaken naive new feeling and expectation. Such a scheme appears to do justice to consciousness in its contradictory fullness, and implies a closer working together of the opposites than would any other rendering—which accords with the essay, for Ransom describes an alliance of sorts.

8. John Crowe Ransom, "The Tense of Poetry," in *The World's Body* (Baton Rouge: Louisiana State University Press, 1968), p. 246.

It does so briefly. We cannot believe that the peculiar happiness ascribed to Adam was actual, it says: lacking mental techniques, Adam could not have "a distinguished aesthetic experience. No percept without a concept, sharp percepts mean sharp concepts, rich percepts mean a multiplicity of concepts. . . . The brilliant effect we admire in a poem is the result of compounding many prose effects, and technical or specific ones"; and the task of poetry is to "soften or dissolve" the hard "prose effect" in a whole experience. Yet technique once set upon its course will outrun poetry and threaten to destroy it.[9]

The scientific and other techniques have come to hold a role in the elevation of sensibility distantly similar to that of the social and the artistic forms. They are hard shapes, impressed by the will upon the experiential self, and the result is a more poetic experience. Ransom probably did not intend the likeness, which is tenuous. At the least it complicates matters, since elsewhere *The World's Body* puts science on the side of the ruthless appetites that the forms must tame. Still, the analogy is a tempting one.

Here we will take a look at the poetics of the New Criticism, a huge subject that I shall not presume to add to, since it has a host of more knowledgeable and accomplished analysts. Its essence, in the treatment given it by Ransom and Tate, seems to be the defining of good poetry as a tension between two elements. On the one side is the story the poem tells, or its rational idea, or the universal class of real objects to which belongs the specific thing the poet

9. Ibid., pp. 241–42.

describes. This is the element in the poem that most quickly lends itself to paraphrase. On the other side is what Ransom in "Criticism, Inc." calls the "tissue" of the poem, or its "irrelevance"—irrelevant, that is, to efficient abstract logic: the whole tangle of imagery and association and rich wording. The tissue individualizes the object with which the poem deals, Ransom says; it keeps the object from fading into the universal that is its type.[10] Tate has used another set of terms for approximately the same elements. The "tension" of a poem, explains "Tension in Poetry" (1938), is the strain between its "*extension*," its literal statement or its announcement of a universal, and its "*intension*," or metaphor and suggestiveness.[11] We would expect both critics to be interested more in the "tissue" or "intention" than in the literal, rationalist element. Ransom, indeed, seems to place his sympathies with the tissue of the poem, where the object is rescued from its universal. But Tate, in a respectful essay on Hart Crane, has emphasized the importance in a great philosophical or epic poem of its firmly articulated idea. "When the poet extends his perception, there is a further extension of the groundwork ready to meet it and discipline it, and to compel the sensibility of the poet to stick to the subject. It is a game of chess; neither side can move without consulting the other." Tate can even regret that modern poets play only with the chessmen of

10. John Crowe Ransom, "Criticism, Inc.," in *The World's Body*, p. 348.
11. Allen Tate, "Tension in Poetry," in *Collected Essays*, p. 83.

sensibility.[12] Both critics would demand, though, that however strong the two elements in the poem may be, however resistant to each other, and however splendid, therefore, the triumph of the poet in composing them into a single work, the result must be an indivisible whole—not a philosophical or moral declaration made persuasive by a garnishing of images, but a declaration that is in the images. A consequence is that poetry takes on a dual meaning. Ransom's aesthetic doctrine would make the poem, along with other artistic works, a respectful and sensitive approach to an object lying outside it. Now, however, it is as though the poem itself also has taken on the character of an object, possessing in its rational idea the structure and coherence that an object has and in its wording and images the massive particularity. In "Three Types of Poetry" (1934), Tate says of *Macbeth* that it is "neither true nor false, but *exists as a created object.*" [13]

What I want to suggest, at any rate, is a likeness between the land that Tate and Ransom as Agrarians describe and the poetic object (whether the poem itself or the object it refers to) that they consider as New Critics. Both the poem and the land, in the presentation our Southerners give of them, have an essentially tactile character, a stubborn concreteness and irreducibility; both possess wholeness and bring something of it to us. But—and I think the two critics would be quick to acknowledge the

12. Allen Tate, "Hart Crane," in *Collected Essays*, pp. 230–31.

13. Allen Tate, "Three Types of Poetry," in *Collected Essays*, p. 109.

contradiction—the land of the Agrarians is an innocent wholeness, and received by its dwellers with
simplicity, while much of the modern fiction and
poetry that interests some of the New Critics is tortu-
ously "dialectical," a wholeness painstakingly con-
structed, and the New Criticism itself is a complex
dialectical engagement of literature. In literature,
then, the poet or critic sets the methods of our time
to overcoming themselves and restoring a measure
of the unity and particularity that once were available.

The World's Body does not identify in a limiting
way the nature or location of the loved object—as it
should not, for its doctrine ought to imply a world
full of good things to be cherished; perhaps Ransom
would admit the work of art to a place among them,
as a particular intricate state of being that was
dreamed of and then realized by its artist lover. We
might think of the poem or painting, if it is not of a
literalist character, as tracing for us some special
state that has only a potential and not a fulfilled objective life until the artistic work has delineated it.
Both of these suggestions, in denying that the beloved object must necessarily be fully existing in
space and time before the artist has come to it, pull
Ransom's poetics very far. They carry the risk of
setting the poet upon a path of romantic self-explora-
tion and self-expression, which is precisely what
Tate and Ransom would not want; but much of their
critical apparatus remains to hold the poet to a more
sober and exacting course. He is still required to be
faithful to the specifications of the particular event,
to discover it in its particularity, even if it is an event

that lives first in his intuition; and he still must compound into a single effect his rational conception and his lyric detail.

The point is that we should be hesitant to exclude any one kind of thing from being a possible candidate for poetic object. This should mean that the offerings of science, too, may present themselves as candidates. Ransom has since spoken kindly of science and technology, in terms reminiscent of the argument in "The Tense of Poetry"; they are, he indicates, disruptions of innocent experience in the interest of getting at least the environment and instrumentalities for more elaborate experience.[14] In *The World's Body* he was insisting on a distinction between the poetic mentality and the scientific, which is concerned only with the "universals." But the art work, for all the thickness its detail gives it, may be radically and intentionally an abstraction in its contrast with the thicker objective world—the sparest of forms, picked out by severely chosen details, and triumphant as much in its purity of form as in its feeling for substantiality. And cannot the scientific formula be, in its own spareness, an invitation to touch the substantial world upon which its lines are sketched?

Allen Tate published in 1938 a splendid novel that places the social and aesthetic vision in a living circumstance. The setting of *The Fathers* is Virginia and Georgetown at the breaking up of the Union. The story is told through the elderly Lacy Buchan's

14. John Crowe Ransom, "Art and the Human Economy," *The Kenyon Review* VII: 4 (Autumn, 1945): 686.

recollections of his boyhood. His father, Major Lewis Buchan, sums up the antebellum Southern social order. George Posey, who marries Lacy's sister Susan, reflects the modern temperament; as a destructive presence in the Buchan family, he is an instance of the forces that were beating in upon the Old South. In Major Buchan, substantial feeling and moral will are one. He is a whole man and a gentleman; he gets his gentlemanly completeness from his perfect relationship to a full and sustaining environment, though it is on the verge of crumbling. He exemplifies the Southerner whose character, Tate had said in *Stonewall Jackson,* is in his property—and that can mean also in the kin and community within which his property locates itself. The Buchans, remembers the narrator, seemed to suffer their domestic troubles and the political crisis as a single event, for "as in all highly developed societies the line marking off the domestic from the public life was indistinct." [15] The community contains manners and ceremonies for the expression of the important feelings, and the "personal" sphere as we know it hardly exists, or hardly articulates itself. The moral and emotional lives of the antebellum Virginians, acted out through precise community rituals and customs, become in effect impersonal and have dignity. Deep in grief at the death of his wife, the major allows the funeral to be the public statement of the loss; his own part in the proceedings is simply to be polite and considerate to those who are attending. Later, his Virginia society

15. Allen Tate, *The Fathers,* introduction by Arthur Mizener (Chicago: The Swallow Press, Sage Books, 1960), p. 125.

pursuing a secession he deplores and his own family falling apart, the major writes Lacy a letter that—so Tate seems to say—could come only from someone who joins the private to the public order and lives ceremoniously within the dense and mannerly composite, ceremoniously restrained even in his revelation of his own distress. His son Semmes has defied him and stood by disunionism, "whereupon I said, reluctantly and without passion, that he was no longer a son of mine"; but instead of giving himself over to the story of the rift, as a modern person would do, Buchan tells of it quietly toward the end of a letter discussing family affairs and Lee's decision to go with Virginia.[16]

George Posey, although of an established family, has been raised outside the system of understandings that have perfectly tempered the major. George must be personal, and shape himself through his own will and passions. Tate might have said of him that he lives by the angelic imagination, trying to grasp the essences by an autonomous thrust of the will, as the major lives by the symbolic imagination and contents himself with the truths his surroundings provide him. George, whose reckless vitality attracts Lacy and Semmes, scorns the major's world and longs for it. What he wants, fretfully and almost unconsciously, from the Buchans, besides Susan, is a context within which he can act beyond his own personality: "while that world existed, its piety, its order, its elaborate rigamarole—his own forfeited heritage—teased him like a nightmare" of dreams

16. Ibid., pp. 175–77.

within dreams. "All violent people secretly desire to be curbed by something that they respect, so that they may become known to themselves." [17] A romantic would predict a heroic future for feelings and a will that are free of social order; but George's, while forceful, have little power of direction and growth. His will is energetic, but it is the energy of spasm rather than of consistent purpose. His feelings have violence without depth or perception. He is intemperate in his love of Susan and inattentive to her; his appetite for existence is restless, and it has not the keenness to relish a sight of rippling green crops. George represents what Ransom's essays imply, the alliance between the apparent opposites of science and primitive lust, for in his eagerness to seize upon existence George reduces it by cold rationality to its usable terms. The lands and yields that a more civilized person would enjoy for themselves mean to him so much cash value; and while disapproving of slavery, he is too practical to refrain from selling slaves.

George's boyhood Georgetown home suggests the sickness, which seems at once a hypertrophy and an atrophy, of feelings that drift outside a social milieu. Having abandoned the duties and amenities that brought Southern ladies into the sunlight of social existence, his mother and her sister have retreated to dusty refinement, an obsession with the private minutiae of their separate lives. In the same dark home lives George's uncle, Mr. Jarman Posey, breathing a musty air of literature and fantasy, a

17. Ibid., p. 180.

recluse like Poe's Roderick Usher: "Poe had a prophetic insight—for Mr. Jarman, like Usher, had had
so long an assured living that he no longer knew that
it had a natural source in human activity; and I suppose he began from his early manhood to retire upon
himself." [18] Mr. Jarman Posey has fallen into that
disease of abstraction our critics have warned about.
Speaking a stilted literary English in place of the
traditional gentleman's English with its "ain't," he
converses in high generalities.[19]

The Fathers is a stunning novel, and a remarkable testing out of social philosophy in an imagined
living situation. It is in one way a curious accom-
plishment. Its author has been a spokesman for a
literary school that has sounded, perhaps not quite
by its own intention, almost as though it would deny
to ideas the right to have an explicit independent
place within an artistic work. The most admirable
figure, Major Buchan, is a gentleman in whom
thought is totally contained within tradition, manners, and experience. Yet ideas command The Fathers: careful speculative observations made by the
narrator on the events he recalls give the themes,
and the characters are representations of them.
While Tate has a pleasing skill at bringing back the
texture of life in an era that is past and peopling it
with real human beings, it is the ideas that give the
novel its greatest strength.

The sensibility possessed by Major Buchan is
indivisible. His exquisitely polished manners, his

18. Ibid., p. 178.
19. Ibid., pp. 232–35, 256.

spareness of open gesture, his impersonality—the traits that in another person would be the results of reason and a strenuous moral will—derive in Buchan's case from that brand of feeling we call taste and from the massive feeling that constitutes his sense of his social heritage. Ransom's civilized technician of the feelings as we may imagine him from "The Tense of Poetry" has a stature of another sort. He has risked experience by assigning it to the hands of reason, its potential enemy, but has thereby increased its varieties. Can it not be said that in compelling himself to the subtle rigorous tasks of shaping forms upon experience and resisting its immediate demands, he has gained a special dignity of will?

❀   ❀   ❀   ❀

Ransom would be the slightest bit uncomfortable with that. He has disliked the unlovely business of the moralists and shown little wish to see the will or the conscience launch itself, with stiff-jawed earnestness, upon its own enterprises against the tug of memory and feeling. A more explicit splitting up of the consciousness into moral-part and emotion-part and a more thorough recommendation of the moral project are to be found in the writings of a critic who was in his late sixties when *I'll Take My Stand* appeared.

Paul Elmer More generally is identified with a school of philosophical and literary opinion that came to be termed the *New Humanism*. Denouncing form-

experiencing of it, the substantiality and harmonious-ness and joy of the flesh.

More's writings today have an air of pleasant quaintness. We are taken into conversation with a vanishing, if not vanished, species: the Gentleman and Man of Letters, the humane scholar, who moves in easy intimacy through the range of literature from the classics to modernity, from the Hindus to the West. In some of his essays he will talk about the books and poems he has read, sketching the life of an author, listening to a poem or two, determining the characteristic flavor and commitment of the artist's work. A good proportion of the pieces in the Shelburne Essays, issued in eleven series from 1904 to 1921, are of this kind. Elsewhere More turns directly to philosophical and religious speculation. A tone of high philosophical seriousness runs through the whole of More's writing, including the literary essays, but the later productions are the most ex-tensively philosophical.

The Greek Tradition, a study of Greek and early Christian thought, came out in four volumes: The Religion of Plato (1921), Hellenistic Philosophies (1923), The Christ of the New Testament (1924), and Christ the Word (1927). It was preceded by Platonism, a set of lectures delivered in 1917 and projected as an introduction to the larger study, and followed up by The Catholic Faith, which appeared in 1931. Taken together, the six volumes are an argument for Platonic dualism and for a Christianity that contains the perfect religious statement of dualism in its paradox, the Word is made flesh. More's position is given more succinctly in The

Sceptical Approach to Religion, published in 1934
and listed as the second volume of the New Shelburne Essays (the first volume, *The Demon of the
Absolute,* was published in 1928 and the third, en-
titled *On Being Human,* in 1936). In the middle
1920s More wrote a piece that was issued in 1937
under the title *Pages from an Oxford Diary.* It is a
fictional reflection by a narrator who has thought and
felt his way to a Platonic Christianity and it bears
evidence of a quietly impassioned quest. In 1935
More and Frank Leslie Cross put out, under the title
of *Anglicanism,* a large collection of seventeenth-
century Anglican religious literature. It is most
particularly to the Anglican faith that More's later
writing looks.

The controlling term in More's philosophical
speculations is *dualism.* Our apprehension of dualism, he insists, does not come primarily from reason,
which in its arrogance will try to replace the dualistic
paradox by a unity more agreeable to neat logic.
Rather, the confirmation of dualism depends upon a
larger reasonableness. It can begin with recognizing
the simplest dualism, that of mind and matter. But
the polarity of mind and objects exists, in turn,
within a cosmic dualism in which spirit or Ideas
confront the whole mutable world; in that confronta-
tion mind stands with the world, at opposites to the
Ideas.[22]

Within a dualistic cosmos, the claims of the
spirit are unquestionably primary. Will the superior

22. Paul Elmer More, *The Christ of the New Testament*
(Princeton: Princeton University Press, 1924), pp. 6, 13–14.

man or woman therefore join the mystics in retreating from our gross and mutinous earth-world to the pure realm of spirit and Ideas? Much of More's writing will leave the reader undecided as to what value he would place on the mystic renunciation. Surely he reveals throughout his essays a relish for the goods of the world, more especially for poetry and the other gentle and elegant elements of civilized life. You do find in "Delphi and Greek Literature," an early essay published in the Second Series of the Shelburne Essays (1905), the pronouncement on the Hindus that, for all their magnificent courageous attempt to break into the otherworld, "life is not of the spirit alone. The body which they so insolently neglected had its revenge." [23] We are left uncertain, though, whether More actually intends to elevate the earth about us to a full legitimacy, or whether he would merely mean to acknowledge that for most human beings a chaste and disciplined residence in the world, however short that may come of the highest state, is the most that is attainable without physical and mental collapse.

The later writings, with their triumphant affirmation that the Word is made flesh, give the firm answer: we are to live in this world as well as beyond it. One construction that has been placed upon the mystic's refusal to love the creature would

23. Paul Elmer More, "Delphi and Greek Literature," in Shelburne Essays, 11 vols. (New York: Phaeton Press, 1967), Second Series, p. 217. (The earliest collections of the Shelburne Essays were not assigned overall titles. As the series progressed, however, titles were added to the editions).

claim that in turning from the creaturely attributes and qualities to the pure "substance" of spirit, the mystic finds his way back to love of his fellow human beings—except that now he loves their real selves, their "substance." To this, More exclaims: "What meaning adheres to a 'naked substance' stripped of all the qualities which denote the mind and heart and character of a living individual creature, that we should love it?" [24]

The precariousness of our place in this dual existence More describes in a passage that favorably summarizes the explanation of evil given by the early Christian theologian Athanasius. The world, goes this concept in More's articulation of it, was called forth by the logos, to be a flawless dwelling for human beings possessing pure souls. The true end of man as a "logical" being—a being not only informed by the logos but conscious of possessing it [25] —is to contemplate the things of the spirit. But man, like other creatures, is mutable; unlike them, he has free will. This compound of mutability and will, wherein lies man's honor, holds also his peril. For the "true motion" of the soul, "towards what is akin to its nature but ever beyond its perfect comprehension, requires a continuity of attention and energy not easy for a creature of whose very essence mutability is a constituent"; and the soul always tends therefore toward reluctance and slackness, a lapse into "the

24. Paul Elmer More, *The Catholic Faith* (Princeton: Princeton University Press, 1931), p. 278.

25. Paul Elmer More, *Christ the Word* (New York: Greenwood Press, 1969), p. 281.

less exacting contemplation" of itself and its bodily activities.[26]

The Platonic equivalent of this, as it is found in More's writing, discovers a tension between the Ideas, which are to give shape to the world, and some primal dissolute tendency on the world's part to resist their work. More distinguishes among the Ideas. The "mere *universalia* of logic," those general Ideas that correspond to individuals, as the Idea table corresponds to particular tables, have no opposites—the Idea man differs from the Idea horse, but is not an opposite—and call for no decision from us. It is the ethical and aesthetic Ideas, set against real contraries—the Idea goodness against evil, the Idea beauty against ugliness—that make their plea for our allegiance.[27] These we must serve, or we shall crumble into the sloth and derangement that is the world's tendency and ours. This belief in the presence of pure and simple Ideas that calls us at every moment from the downward drag of the world brings with it, I think, a bracing freedom to complement its moral rigorousness; for if purity sits in perpetual judgment on our present situation, then we are not bound to the particulars of that situation, as the logic of Agrarianism might imply. Instead we are free and commanded to reconstruct it in accordance with the models the moral imagination provides.

We are to confirm our world along with the

26. Ibid., pp. 292–94.
27. *The Catholic Faith*, pp. 150–51; Paul Elmer More, "Platonic Idealism," in *The Sceptical Approach to Religion*, New Shelburne Essays, vol. II (Princeton: Princeton University Press, 1934), pp. 63–65.

kingdom of the spirit and mediate between them in the service of the spiritual things. That is the clear conviction More had arrived at by the time he had finished his multivolume study of Greek and Christian thought; it is given more ambivalent statement in the earlier parts of that work. It is, therefore, puzzling to come upon a passage in *The Christ of the New Testament* that seems to exalt the ascetic way of withdrawal above the middling ways of a decent worldliness. To turn the other cheek, More writes in the troublesome passage, to receive all borrowers, to give up your cloak when your coat has been seized, are not practical rules for a civilization of property and police; but Jesus meant them literally. More urges merely that we be honest and clearheaded with ourselves as to which morality we are choosing, the higher morality expressed in the literal command of Jesus or the lower morality holding the world to some approximation of Christian goodness. If we choose the lower, we should strive "always to rise to the plane that lies just above." [28]

Do the creature-world and the mediating strategies appropriate to it fall short here of the full honor *The Catholic Faith* will pay them; is More relegating them to a human majority incapable of anything better? Something like this may be the case. More's language so often strains toward otherworldliness as to warrant the guess that the ascetic renunciation remained until very late an exemplar for him of the spiritual life, an alternative to which he could almost absentmindedly turn even when his

28. *The Christ of the New Testament*, pp. 136–39.

explicit philosophy and theology were moving toward rejecting it. We could, however, reconcile the passage with a belief in a perfect morality of exact mediation between spirit and world, as opposed to a perfect morality of withdrawal from the world. While a mendicant's gift of his last coat to a freezing man, for example, may represent the mystical intention of abandoning the world and its dross, the gift may represent to the contrary the assurance that the world's warmth and comfort are genuine goods to be given to others. In that case it is at once affirmation and discipline of the flesh, a mediating between flesh and spirit.

That a morality of mediation might be perfect rather than compromising in its interior severity and integrity is the implication of a comment in More's "The Spirit of Anglicanism," which champions the quality of temperance, of measure, in Anglican religion. More turns to "Aristotle's definition of the ethical mean as both a limit and unlimited": courage, for instance, is a "measured avoidance" of two excesses, cowardice and rashness; "but in itself, as a motive of conduct, it has its own direction to which there is no limit." No such thing exists as an excess of courage or of any other virtue.[29] Now both moralities, the renunciatory and the mediating, might have an imperfect and compromising as well as a perfect

29. Paul Elmer More, "The Spirit of Anglicanism," in *Anglicanism: The Thought and Practice of the Church of England, Illustrated from the Religious Literature of the Seventeenth Century,* compiled and edited by Paul Elmer More and Frank Leslie Cross (Milwaukee, Wisconsin: Morehouse Publishing Company, 1935), p. xxiii.

level. The Christian who believes in the flight from the world, but cannot practice it, might reason: "If I were a perfect Christian I would shun all earthly things; but I am not perfect, and so I will involve myself with this world, but only those portions of it that have been subjugated to justice, mercy, or Christian art." And the Christian who believes in a perfect mediation between the spirit and the world but is unequal to that exquisitely demanding task might conclude: "If I were a perfect Christian I would live exactly at the point at which earth and spirit meet: I would obey the command of the spirit by refusing property over any good thing, and I would celebrate the world by rejoicing at my neighbor's pleasure in sharing the earth's goods over which I have relinquished control. But I am not a perfect Christian, nor are my fellows; so I am going to accept, for myself and others, the selfish worldliness of private property, but work to propagate a system of property that is just and productive." If it is this second way of distinguishing between a perfect and an imperfect morality that we can imagine to be operating in *The Christ of the New Testament,* the passage is in full concordance with More's later confident embracing of the world as it is redeemed in the spirit.

More was a moralist in every fiber; he associated morality with a tense exercise of the will, and much of the implication his "dualism" carries has to do with this concept of the moral life. To describe the cosmos as dualistic is to say that the parts of an individual existence, if it is morally perceived and lived, do not flow easily together; the will has elected, over and over, to strain against some insistent tendency of life in the interest of some superior but less clamoring one. The conduct and even the intuitional source of morality and the spiritual life will be stark. Few if any images are to be found in More's work of a morality that is impulsive, emotional, and expansive. He can suggest the rapture of the philosopher who has a glimpse of the Ideas in their purity; he can claim in "Definitions of Dualism," an essay in *The Drift of Romanticism* (1913), that a moral existence is attended by "happiness," a condition of assurance and self-approval to be clearly distinguished from the lower and worldly though legitimate experience of pleasure;[30] yet the moral and spiritual existence itself he identifies with a state he defines by the sober phrase, the "inner check."

The inner check in More's understanding is something like an impulse, if the word *impulse* can be separated from its connotation of the visceral and emotional. It is an immediate halt, nearly automatic for the morally disciplined individual, in the working out of a desire, a distancing of yourself from the desire so that you can get free of its power and make some judgment about it. Notice that the inner check does not necessarily rule against emotion and desire. The judgment may be favorable in the particular case, More writes in *Platonism,* and then you can proceed with the desire, which will now, I imagine, be trimmer and more comely—and even

30. Paul Elmer More, "Definitions of Dualism," in *The Drift of Romanticism,* Shelburne Essays, Eighth Series, pp. 252–54.

possibly more conscious and exquisite, though More might hesitate at the suggestion of so hedonistic a thing—than when it first came to you. Still, the passage in which More allows the inner check to grant expression to some desires goes on to imply a steady progress, on the part of the person who constantly exercises the check, from specific desires to the contemplation of higher and more encompassing Ideas, and the reader gathers that in time the whole life of desire for worldly pleasures will fall behind. Possibly More in 1917 was still somewhat under the spell of an otherworldly kind of Idealism. The passage remains [31] in a revised edition published in 1926 and reissued in 1931; but I believe it would be more conformable to More's later thought to presume that the inner check will not lead us out of this world, but will transform our acting relations with the world.

The reality of the inner check is believable. More may in part be pointing to an easily recognized situation, the perverse penchant of conscience for turning almost automatically quarrelsome toward the desires to which we especially wish to submit. But More might not be quite satisfied with that statement of the case. The conscience it describes does not have exactly the requisite coolness. The inner check More talks of is spare, temperate, and questioning. It serves the vision of an ordered cosmos and it approves of harmoniousness, proportion, economy. And More wants a conscience that will restrain even its

31. Paul Elmer More, *Platonism*, The Louis Clark Vanuxem Foundation Lectures for 1917–1918, rev. ed. (Princeton: Princeton University Press, 1926), pp. 201–4.

own more aggressive ambitions for mastery. He places a prideful asceticism among the many projects that represent the exalting of self-will over self-restraint, the urge to identify personal inclination with higher authority. The ascetic, More says, is someone "who translates the inhibitions of the spirit into a positive law of physical discomfort." [32]

Morality, though, involves specific thoughts and acts, and for these a discipline of mere inhibition seems a peculiar basis. But the inner check, according to More, is normally or often the prelude to a moral choice among impulses, a choice that can be exercised because the individual has put a brief stop to the urgency of some particular impulse. In "Definitions of Dualism," we read that the act of "attention," of choosing an impulse, comes immediately with the halt of the rival impulse. The result is that the inner check and the choice appear synonymous.[33] Since morality as we know it constantly requires the overcoming of some rival impulse called up by fear, possessiveness, or the like, it is easy enough to see how the model of the inner check can provide a description of positive moral activity. The impulse "checked" may be the urge to stay frozen with fright or clutched to our possessions; the "check" may issue in all sorts of courageous and self-giving acts. By now we seem to be burdening our analysis of morality with a cumbersome machinery of checks and propulsions; why can we not simply concede to the actively courageous person the active

32. Ibid., pp. 282–85.
33. "Definitions of Dualism," in *The Drift of Romanticism*, pp. 250–51.

virtue of courage and to the sacrificing the gift of compassion? A responding argument for the concept of the inner check might be that it brings its own kind of economy in presenting the moral will, as More would want it presented, in its most severe aspect, uncolored by sentimental emotion.

The clearest demand that the inner check meets is that of resisting, in the cause of the Ideas or the spirit, the nihilistic urges of the mutable world. But the will has additional effort to expend. In the essay "A Scholar-Saint," More commends the religious thought of Baron von Hügel for its emphasis on the "costingness" of the religious life. Religion, More observes, can require either of two costs. It may require the ascetic renunciation of all worldly things. "Or it may exact the sacrifice of ease for such a strenuous unremitting control of temperamental impulse towards either pole of tension"—the spiritual or the worldly—"as is needed for mediation and adjustment." More defines the second program as the humanist one. Asceticism may seem to levy the heavier payment, he remarks, but measured in "energy of the will" the humanist way could prove the more demanding.[34]

On one level the "costingness" of humanism as More presents that discipline amounts to holding out against two temptations: the unmistakable temptation of the flesh and the finer temptation to break with the world and seek the purity of the spirit.

34. Paul Elmer More, "A Scholar-Saint," in *On Being Human*, New Shelburne Essays, vol. III (Princeton: Princeton University Press, 1936), pp. 167–68.

More clearly believed that, despite all the agony of self-mortification the mystical project imposes on its Western practitioners, it is enticing to certain temperaments of deeply religious cast. Put this way, the argument will win from most of us little more than an intellectual assent. We know that ascetic mystics have lived, and that they spoke with longing and with ecstasy. But when More talks of abandoning all pleasant earthly things as though it could express a "temperamental impulse," to be resisted with strength of character for the sake of a moderate commerce with the world's goods, he is defining a phenomenon that refuses to connect up with anything in our normal experience. A more convincing claim for the "costingness" of More's humanism might contend that the ascetic renunciation may relax the pull of certain "lower" though acceptable desires the humanist must live with in a tense and disciplined manner. To consign yourself, once and for all, to subsisting on a few grains will require a tremendous act of will; but it may conceivably be easier to continue thereafter upon that basis than to eat a rich course every day and push aside a second. I doubt it. Perhaps a safely modest rephrasing would be to say that the humanist, in this case and others, performs a specific kind of daily resistance the ascetic does not engage in. Another way of getting More's argument into accord with common experience would be to relinquish the simple Platonic construction: on that side Idea or spirit, on this side the world. Taken more broadly, the essay can describe a moral will alert and tense and discriminating among all the conflicting possibilities of life. A moral tension of this sort recalls Irving Babbitt's report of Pascal's distinction between the abstract *esprit de géométrie* and the *esprit de finesse,* a deftness at making judgments about the details of living, judgments resting upon "such a multitude of delicate perceptions" that often the judge cannot give a logical explanation of them. This *esprit de finesse,* of course, has a lightness that may set it a little apart from anything so formidable as the moral will, and one of its products is a "fine tact." [35] But like the moral will we may detect in "A Scholar-Saint" if we set aside the simplest kind of Platonic model, it is deftly critical and disciplined to nuances within an existence not merely dual (although Babbitt apparently liked an Aristotelian dualism) but multifaceted.

The emphasis upon the flinty hardness of the moral enterprise relates to an interest on More's part whose results a reader might consider the most ambiguous of all his efforts. In the cause of austerity, of Platonism, of Christianity, More does battle with a thing he calls "humanitarianism," which appears to include the romantic definition of man as possessed of a simple spontaneous goodness, and the romantic identification of morality with an emotional impulse toward goodness. The whole modern social reformist movement in More's judgment sprang from these or similar notions. More's insistence on the difference between "humanitarianism" and Christianity is important, but much of its importance lies in a fact imperfectly explored in his writing. To get a perception

35. *Rousseau and Romanticism,* pp. 35–36.

of Christian love as a clear, hard, and absolute imperative that does not ride upon the more pleasant emotions or upon some sentimental view of those who are to be loved means that it can retain its power to judge and correct the easier definitions of love and the easier programs of social justice.

More does talk briefly to the point. Using "imagination" to signify roughly the ability to see an existence outside ourselves, see and feel it as an actual reality, More associates imagination and Christian love in such manner as to suggest their exacting discipline: "Love, as we define it, would be that outreaching power of the imagination by which we grasp and make real to ourselves the being of others"—the precise being of a specific person.[36] Whether love leads to this understanding or the understanding to the love is of secondary importance at the moment. What More gives us basically is a description of a consciousness naked and exact in its awareness of our fragile fellow human beings; and this state of consciousness should be the foundation for a social activism that refuses to abstract one group into the Oppressed and another into Oppressors, or otherwise to reduce the multiplicity of human character and need to ideological terms. To phrase that more realistically: we would have a continuing process in which love and conscience, incessantly slipping into the convenient abstract social creeds and delicious moral indignations we legitimately rely on in our inconstancy of will, are incessantly recalled to the perfect imperative they must try to imitate.

36. *The Christ of the New Testament*, pp. 123–26.

More does not fix upon this reasonable implication of his own thought. Instead of attempting to come to terms with "humanitarianism" in his inclusive use of the phrase, as the fallible approximation of the Christian imperative, requiring a ruthless criticism of itself precisely because it is healthy and promising enough to deserve the corrective of criticism, More simply dismisses it, or nearly so—a passage in "The New Morality," an essay in *Aristocracy and Justice* (1915), does praise his humanitarian age for its sensitivity to suffering and its banishment of much cruelty.[37] More's prescription comes down to this formula: for those who can follow the command of Christ, a life of poverty and giving; for the rest of mankind, a life shaped by some institutions, notably property, that provide a just and decently prosperous social order. This just but imperfect social state is, to be sure, the shadowed image of a perfect Christianity. But it operates also by its own economic laws of efficient production, More contends in "The Religious Ground of Humanitarianism," a piece included in the First Series of the Shelburne Essays; and he warns that any attempt to impose a perfect sharing upon imperfect society will merely overthrow those laws, and with bad result.

The effect of the argument virtually is to seal off our workaday society from any ultimate and active judgment that a Christian community might make upon it. Instead of living our imperfect social and economic existence with the ruthlessly pressing example before us of a perfect poverty and self-

37. Paul Elmer More, "The New Morality," in *Aristocracy and Justice,* Shelburne Essays, Ninth Series, p. 209.

giving—so that if we must have some selfish amass-
ing of private property beyond the owner's need and
the need of any dependents we shall at least col-
lectively cultivate a disturbed conscience at the
excess—all of us who do not choose poverty are to go
ahead and accumulate as much as we can, confident
that we are indirectly improving an imperfect world
on its own imperfect terms. More would, of course,
have business and government stand at the bar of
Christianity for any actual injustices and inhumani-
ties they commit. It is reasonable enough to assume
that an individual who fulfills in his own person,
and labors at establishing among his fellows, even the
minimal requirements of justice has undertaken a
considerable moral task. More may be going further
than this, and holding as his ideal of the good
Christian property owner a person who ministers
his or her wealth daily for the benefit of the community, dwelling among possessions with the austerity of a mendicant. But an individual who so acts is
living the fact, if not the form, of Christian poverty
anyway; we would have no necessity of differentiat-
ing a higher poverty from a lower decent affluence.

The plain drift of More's thought on the subject
is to set up two Christian orders, one the direct
expression of Christ's command and the other a mere
mundane shadow of Christian perfection, and set
them on almost separate careers. It is a teasing devia-
tion from More's ethic, which usually posits a sterner
and more varied dealing between perfection and our
perpetually downward-sloping lives.[38] The argument

38. *The Christ of the New Testament*, p. 139.

may reflect a persistence of More's early leaning toward an otherworldly mysticism as well as his distaste for radical reform, and represent a distinction between a mystical life in rejection of the world, on the one hand, and on the other a worldly life among creaturely things. More's later abandonment of the distinction would then make possible a more restless social philosophy holding worldly society to be capable of receiving the full print of the spirit, and therefore judging it more closely for its fallings from the spirit.

A sample of how More can look at social reform is provided by an essay on William Morris that is included in the Seventh Series (1910). That nineteenth-century British artist and reformer, with his socialism, his nostalgia for medieval England, his practice of the handcrafts, his fanciful poems and fiction recalling old graceful heroic times to life, provides More with a good occasion for his own rugged, no-nonsense biases. He treats Morris with not inconsiderable respect, but finds him to be of a liquid, impatient temperament incapable of settling itself upon a specific fact—the species of temperament that More would identify with romanticism. More can admire Morris for his efforts to revive good, joyful craftsmanship in its various branches. What he thinks lacking in Morris's poetic art is caught in this comment on *The Earthly Paradise:* "beauty is only the indistinguished blaze of gold and silver, lilies and roses, slender hands and white limbs. Nowhere is there any relief or emphasis"; there is only "an even, swift flow, which never invites the mind to pause, or reflect, or go back." For *News from Nowhere,* Morris's vision of a utopia without laws, of gentle people delighting in one another, enjoying their crafts, moving from task to task as the whim dictates, More has a predictable impatience. His general criticism of Morris's social thought is essentially the same as the criticism of the poetry: that Morris refused to deal in stubborn, differentiated fact.[39]

The charms of Morris's ideas, the dreams of a life simple and healthy, filled with work that is play, lived by loving creatures who move gracefully through a country landscape, need the balance that a gruff and civilized conservatism like More's can offer. The problem is that the conservatism has just a little of the facile quality More censures in his subject. We scarcely have to be told, as More tells his readers, that the utopia in *News from Nowhere* is not "practical." Of course it is impractical. Morris's fantasy is a bold attempt, by an individual of generous feelings and an experimental bent, to sketch out one possible arrangement of the world's goods and tasks. In substitution for sophisticated political or sociological analysis, it has its own practicality of a sort that political ideologues can lose sight of, a recognition that the good society will have to justify itself by gritty unideological things like gratifying employment and kindly manners. In other endeavors Morris knew the feel of fact: his hands gripped it in weaving and other craft work that required him to learn patient skills against resisting materials. He chose, in an eminently practical way, to make his life an experiment toward a new society—to show that

39. Paul Elmer More, "William Morris," in Shelburne Essays, Seventh Series, pp. 103, 110, 117.

hand work can mean something, to shape the furniture and decoration of homes to a better taste. Actual qualities of temperament—and More may have correctly defined them—stood perhaps against a concentrated intellectual or artistic life that might have resulted in some one more highly finished product. Then we would have had a famous poet or economist: we would not have had the distinctive William Morris, with the special brand of experimentation and disciplined various work he pursued. More's criticism is exact, and a stout antidote to whatever in Morris may have encouraged sentimentality in his readers or followers. But that criticism, insofar as it bears on Morris's social speculations, has a mental provinciality to it, an unwillingness to inquire with the last measure of curiosity and critical alertness into a career that More was convinced must be impractical.

More's lack of inquisitiveness into social issues is especially apparent in "Property and Law," an essay in *Aristocracy and Justice*. Fearing a weakening of will on the issue of property rights, More urges a vigorous, unapologetic assertion of those rights, and a firmer consciousness that civilization depends upon them. The argument could have its point. The proper definition and defense of property is undoubtedly important to conservatism, important possibly to any persuasion that is interested in privacy, independence, and the other benefits associated with ownership. But a careful, friendly examination of property ought to convey some sense of what property specifically is. If, for example, a healthy ownership extends over the physical things that are most intimate to the owner, how shall we define corporate property? William Morris involved himself not exactly with property but with the tools and materials and products that mix themselves into the lives of the craftsmen and their neighbors. The implication of *News from Nowhere* is that these objects are to be divested of absolute ownership and made available to anyone who wants to pick them up for an afternoon's work, but even that amounts to a clear image of objects and their traffic with acting, expressive men and women. But while More's "Property and Law" does make a few fairly specific points, including the contention that we are freed from materialism, freed to take up intangible concerns, only when property as the material basis of our life is safe,[40] the essay in the main does not deal with those loved or usable little chunks of the world that we call property; its subject is Property—it has almost exactly the abstractness Tate has claimed to discover in More's literary opinion. More effortlessly presumes, it appears, that we all know what property is, and that solid good sense argues against attacks on it. We touch here on what may be a characteristic failing on the part of conservatism, a failing that has a counterpart at the opposite political pole. Just as the left, precisely because it knows itself to be the party of compassion, is tempted to slide along a little easily on that self-definition with no real alertness to the moral ambiguities on the left, the passings from moral compassion to moral ferocity, so conservatism

40. Paul Elmer More, "Property and Law," in *Aristocracy and Justice,* p. 146.

with its habitual liking for practicality and limitation tends to believe in its practical sense too trustingly, and to fall into an easy and unanalytical tough-talk.

The essay "Criticism" presents a more persuasive version of More's cultural conservatism. His subject is the spiritual and intellectual heritage of a civilization rather than its material assets; the topic is more congenial to his talent. "We are born," he writes, "into an inheritance of great emotions." We cannot experience these emotions exactly as they were: the martyr's at the stake, the hero's in triumph, and all the other grand emotions out of the past; "but on the other hand with this loss of separate reality they are associated with life as a whole, and in that unity of experience obtain, what they lacked before, a significance and design." It is a mission of criticism and scholarship to select, interpret, and mold together into some "unity of experience" these past experiences.[41] Here is a full and sensitive conservatism, cherishing the past, sensing it as a larger environment in which we move, exact yet free and critical in scrutinizing the past and putting its separate emotions into a usable unity.

So far, More has pictured a universe in which spirit, Idea, logos commands shape upon a reluctant or rebellious creature-world; he has elevated the strenuous will that serves the logos. The world has mostly played secondary parts: it is the context in which the spirit acts, it sets up the resistances the moral will must strain against, and in counterpoint

41. Paul Elmer More, "Criticism," in Shelburne Essays, Seventh Series, pp. 238–44.

with the spiritual realm it supplies complexities and paradoxes for the will to mediate. Listening to what I have just written, I find the abstraction, the implicit capital letters for "Will" and "Spirit," that Tate's commentary would prepare us to expect in More's work—though More could write with a simple grace that gives a concreteness his doctrines do not always provide on their own. He can be read, however, in another way that brings him closer to the concerns, if not the solutions, Tate and Ransom have spoken for. In this reading the world leaps, at the touch of the logos and the grasp of human will, from flux and possibility into a solid and joyful object. The issue now is nearly that of the Agrarians: how shall the fullness of our world be preserved; how shall forms protect and enhance the object? We find suggestions for the question and its answers in More's writing, often scattered, not bound thematically together. But always the ultimate service is of the world to the spirit, and only in that service can the world find its own fulfillment.

A fine passage in *Christ the Word* sets forth the world as the ancient theologians saw it, filled and aglow with logos. The plants and animals, with their adjustments of parts and the adaptation between them and their environments, possessed of a beauty beyond any seeming need for their own existence, bespeak a forming and controlling intelligence. Christ, thought the theologians, was referring to the logos in pointing to the beauty of the unthinking lilies. The "majestic revolution of the stars, the recurrent swell of the tides beneath the moon, and the restraining of the vexed waters of the sea within their bounds," all this manifests the logos. But the phenomenal world is not "logical" in the sense of consciously having logos. That gift is for man; through it he "enters into the life of animals" and understands the actions they perform under the urge of a reason they are not conscious of; he "weighs the stars and measures their orbits"; he sees the beauty of the setting sun and the dawning; the heavens for him have shape and movement. While he sleeps, his mind wanders to adventures and far places. And he is logical not only in private understanding and interior conversation but in the power of language, through which he clothes his thoughts and issues them forth: "logos communes with logos," and man finds himself in a society of logical souls.[42]

The passage is firm and enticing. But as for More's general vision of Ideas that move from the outside in upon formless possibility and work it into form and beauty, the Agrarian alternative remains persuasive. Why, if we are to see a tree as beautiful, do we have to convince ourselves first that it participates in the Idea beauty; why can we not just accept the tree as a very particular good thing, and take whatever concrete and specific experiences its particularity of rough bark and patterned branches has to offer? A good response is one that More, who took his Platonism seriously as philosophical statement, might not have cared for: it is that his Idealism poetically enriches our feeling for existence. We have noted that the concept of a

42. *Christ the Word*, pp. 279–82.

world at contraries suggests the tensions and strategies comprising much of the moral experience. Simi-
larly, More's Platonism could give us a more powerful feeling of the order and comeliness and beauty
that we encounter in the world, a sense that they
do not merely happen within creation but actively
grasp and hold it.

The grasping becomes in one of More's essays
a fact both of the world around us and of the moral
life. "James Joyce" does not look like a promising
essay. At a first reading it is a prudish recoil from
obscenity and the stream of consciousness in Joyce's
work. But beneath the prudery and the unhelpful
critical judgment of Joyce is to be found a provocative essay that attempts to define fundamental ways
of apprehending the world. More appears to be
proposing that obscenity and the abandonment of
the mind to the flux of impressions are closely joined
states, both of them contradicting the compact or-
derliness of creation. He enforces his argument with
a story by R. H. Benson in which a priest, twice
tempted by doubt, is finally tempted to see as il-
lusion even the world of sense. At this, the very materiality of the solid things surrounding him seems
threatened by some nihilistic force.[43] Note how far
away More's thought stands from the simple denun-
ciation of materialism it can sound like. We could
draw out the implication of the essay in this way:
matter as we know it, hard and solid and sharply
differentiated into objects, depends for its existence

43. Paul Elmer More, "James Joyce," in *On Being
Human*, pp. 95–96.

upon the Ideas, which press it tightly into shapes, and depends, for our knowledge and experience of its full materiality, upon our acknowledgment of order, our discipline of the senses to order—in short, upon our moral comprehension. So we arrive at one of the manners in which the moral will, despite or rather because of its oppositeness to the sensuous life in play with the material world, makes that world and that life available to us.

Once again, the best device might be to translate the intellectual construction into experience. You may or may not believe that the world is informed by entities to be named Ideas, and that the moral will owes them allegiance; but you can certainly believe that the world becomes solid and variegated for you in response to affirmative, often difficult acts toward it on your part. This experiencing of the world suggests itself in metaphors. To engage in some work, for example, can yield almost the feeling of pressing against the world as a palpable, a resistant and co-operative fact. The disciplined and delicate use of the senses can be thought of as a carving up of the world into subtle curious objects. Our surroundings, in any event, are substantial and interesting to us, so a moralist might argue, insofar as we confront them with alertness and expectancy. And More's thesis, so extended, comes near to that of John Crowe Ransom, who also offers one or several dualisms of a sort. The civilized forms and disciplines Ransom talks of—he would not have assigned them to the moral will—do their own labor of gripping and differentiation: they seize upon raw, aggressive experience, restrain it from an assault on objects, break it into a more complex sensibility; and civilized man comes to possess, as in More's view of him, a world firm-bodied and varied that mere sensation would never have reported.

While More can suggest in an essay in the Third Series of the Shelburne Essays (1905) that the best poetry comes about when the "discriminating principle works in the writer strongly but unconsciously," when a "certain critical atmosphere" rules the taste without making the poet "dull the edge of impulse by too much deliberation," [44] he would be willing to identify this delicacy of restraint with sharp and angular form. An essay on George Crabbe praises Crabbe for his moral sobriety and his use of the heroic couplet with its clean hard measure, its bitten pause.[45] The impression More gives is that this property in the poet, while praiseworthy mostly for its judiciousness and moral strength, also effects a clearly lined landscape and genre painting in words. Observing in "The Centenary of Longfellow," published in the Fifth Series (1908), that a poem suffers when its lines flow from the poet "too smoothly and fluently," when "they have not been held back long enough to be steeped in the deeper and more obstinate emotions of the breast," More writes that in Longfellow's case the "proper resistance" making for his best poetry usually resulted from "some check imposed by the difficulties of

44. Paul Elmer More, "The Centenary of Sainte-Beuve," in Shelburne Essays, Third Series, pp. 69–70.
45. Paul Elmer More, "George Crabbe," in Shelburne Essays, Second Series, p. 128.
46. Paul Elmer More, "The Centenary of Longfellow," in Shelburne Essays, Fifth Series, p. 145.

form." [46] More is not contradicting himself in discussing sympathetically the aristocratic canon of style and conduct as calling for an appearance of ease.[47] We know how painstaking are the labors of a writer who wants to achieve a conversational ease; but More might find it an even stronger argument for the effect of ease that it connotes the chaste qualities of modesty, economy, proportion, polish, lucidity.

An essay on Anthony Trollope, published in *The Demon of the Absolute,* stoutly affirms the partnership between art and moral conviction. More's opinion of Trollope bases itself implicitly on the belief that our moral judgment of others—moral encounter of them might be a broader and more satisfactory phrasing—is a substantial part of our experience, a way of knowing those around us as real and bodied people. Trollope's open, impassioned, judging involvement in his characters invites the reader, in More's estimate, to participate in the work of judgment and thereby heightens the experiential reality of the story: it intensifies the aesthetic along with the moral effect—or rather, the two effects are nearly identical. And the imaginary world Trollope calls forth is to More's perception dense and sinewy for having will and purpose at its center. "What he held to be desirable, what he presented always as really worthy of respect, was the slow and unostentatious distinction that comes normally to strength of character and steadiness of purpose, checked by the

47. Paul Elmer More, "The Socialism of G. Lowes Dickinson," in Shelburne Essays, Seventh Series, p. 178.

humility of religious conviction." [48] In this essay the moral will comes close to being an emotion rather than a cold opposite to emotion; it appears less as a negative check than as a positive energy.

The case that More makes in the essay on Trollope for the presence of controlling moral thought is not very different from an argument that Lionel Trilling would later present for explicit intellectual statement in literature. In an essay taking issue with the variety of criticism that emphasizes technique and symbol at the expense of intellectual theme, Trilling reports getting from a couplet by Yeats "the pleasure of relevance and cogency," to which both content and rhetoric contribute, and a similar pleasure, kindred to that "involved in responding to a satisfactory work of art," from Freud's *An Outline of Psychoanalysis:* "the pleasure of listening to a strong, decisive, self-limiting voice uttering statements to which I can give assent." [49] Trilling's is as crisp, economical, and persuasive a summing up as the intellectualist position could have. The claim for the literary benefits of committed, informing ideas could actually be brought to the favorable appraisal of More's own work. His predisposition toward philosophy and moral comment appears to have enhanced the freedom and alertness of his

48. Paul Elmer More, "My Debt to Trollope," in *The Demon of the Absolute,* New Shelburne Essays, vol. I (Princeton: Princeton University Press, 1928), pp. 106–8, 119.

49. Lionel Trilling, "The Meaning of a Literary Idea," in *The Liberal Imagination: Essays on Literature and Society* [1950] (Garden City, New York: Doubleday and Company, Anchor Books, 1953), pp. 281–82.

response to literature, the eagerness with which he read, the zest he can awaken in his audience. More's criticisms, to be sure, could be prudish and stiff. The quality I want to define in him is sufficiently limited that it may coexist with a good deal of faulty judgment. It is the ability to pick up a poem or a book and think at it—to find something interesting there, something to pick a courteous quarrel with; and the ability of the critic to pass on this excitement to his audience. By force of his intelligent liking for its balance and abruptness, for example, More can persuade a twentieth-century reader to enjoy the good old heroic couplet. His bias against the romantic fluidity of feeling can intensify our perception of the romantics and our pleasure in them, for it gives clarity and emphasis to that element in their work and leads the reader to a positive, critical experiencing of the romantic emotion.

It is because More came to literature with an equipment of ideas, and a moral dedication to them, that he had a vigorous, questioning responsiveness to the novel or the poem lying before him. The largeness of his ideas and generosity—he seldom failed to find something good in those authors he handled most severely—kept his critical project on the whole from shriveling to the mean dimensions of a more frowning, political variety of moralism. Whatever the reasons, the essays are a pleasure. More ranged with urbane familiarity over an amazing sweep of times and literatures. Some of his essays are filled with engaging detail from the lives of literary figures. He wanted to put a body of work into the personal setting out of which it grew; and he seems to have looked on authors from the past almost as

rhythms and necessities of outer nature—that constitutes for Hannah Arendt the prelude to the
distinctively human enterprise, and some of its
substance. On the other side Paul Goodman, an
elder cousin to the recent counter culture, and
Theodore Roszak, one of its most imaginative sympathetic observers, both seek to define sources of
health that the artificialities of civilization have
stifled. In Goodman's description human consciousness, with its urgent sensuous energies that civilized
conventions constrict, is a rough and contrary thing,
growing into slow self-awareness through specific
working and playing encounters with surroundings
that are circumstantial, particularistic, never more
than partially completed. The more lyrical Roszak
wants a transformation of consciousness, a reawaken-
ing of senses narcotized by science and technology,
so that we may perceive the matter-of-fact universe
as pierced and suffused by transcendent glories.
While modern technology comes out badly in the
work of Arendt and Roszak, in the one case for
signifying our collapse into satisfaction of biological
rhythm and need and in the other for being nature's
enemy, Goodman would put us to mastering a
computer or getting the feel of a machine as he
would introduce us to the myriad other tough and
educative possibilities of our surroundings.

*   *   *   *

The most important of Hannah Arendt's books
for our subject is *The Human Condition*, published

in 1958. It is a work of massive scholarship, but scholarship under an unusual design. The author intends to set forth a vocabulary and set of ideas by which we can understand and judge various elements in the human situation; she draws the words and ideas partly from Western tradition, enticing the utmost meaning she can get from them, and gives to that tradition itself a shape of her own choosing. *The Human Condition* speaks in a compound voice: that of Western civilization, particularly in its Greek and Roman phase, united with the voice of the author. What she proposes with the aid of tradition is that human activity (as distinct from contemplation) should be seen as falling into three classes: the labor that obeys and furthers the organic basis of human existence; work, which builds a distinctively human "world" of artifice; and the speech and action that take place within the political community situated in that world. The proper task of a civilization is to pull itself as far as possible from organic process into the world of artifice and there elevate a politics; this, Arendt finds, her own times have failed to do.

The realm of biological process as described in *The Human Condition* may be thought of as operating on a number of levels: in the rhythms of life that pulse in the body, in the labor and rest and consumption by which the body meets its needs, in the larger rhythms of nature that pace society as a whole. Supplying life itself, the domain of organism offers satisfactions as well. To give yourself to the life movement of effort and rest, of pain and its relaxing, of laboring and consuming, to know your body as it experiences itself in these activities, is to possess a primitive health and joy. The author even warns that the modern means for easing labor —labor being in her terminology the mode of human effort within the realm of biology—robs us of the happiness that comes from the cycle "of exhaustion and regeneration, of pain and release from pain." [1] But these are the simplest terms on which to spend an existence. Biological life is the sphere of the necessities that must be met before humanity is ready for anything else; and if you surrender yourself to the functionings of your body and to the greater biological processes, you are submitting yourself to a necessity that is the denial of freedom. You are deprived of individuality. In the biological realm no one steps forth to show who he is through deeds and words; such an act would go counter to the needs of physical life, which demand a rhythmic, concerted effort by beings who are not distinct individuals but units of labor. The modern biological realm is society, which wants to absorb present-day man. Society is engaged only in the upholding of life; exalting labor, it swarms with human beings who do not stand before one another as individuals, do not perform deeds, but only behave—fall, that is, into predictable patterns—as they labor and consume and labor.

The task of breaking the grip of biology falls to the worker. Labor obeys the process and flow of life, and its products are consumed, dissolved into the process; the worker snatches organic materials from

1. Hannah Arendt, *The Human Condition* (Garden City, New York: Doubleday and Company, Anchor Books, 1959), p. 115.

the life stream and shapes them into enduring objects. Work produces what *The Human Condition* calls "the world": the human artifice, which fills in the spaces between individuals with its objects of stone and wood, and offers their durability against the tempos of the body and the consuming cyclical movements of nature. The objects separate the citizens and relate them. Objects give to human beings and their enterprises some permanence. The objects that are also works of art preserve the memory of deeds and the people who performed them, and they endow the world with beauty. The image I get here is not that the world of artifice intends to overthrow organism and the organic surroundings—on them, after all, every kind of human existence depends, and they are sources of pleasure—but that this world aims to establish its free space in their midst.

Part of the difference that Arendt detects between the laborer's submission to organic processes and the worker's resistance to them has to do with the product: the durable objects made by the worker stand protectively between the human project and the cyclical transformations that rule within nature. But *The Human Condition* points to a difference in subjective experience as well, and this requires some careful definition. Clearly, labor is a sensuous and, in a way, pleasurable expression of organic impulses within the laborer—though the experience is not an easy hedonism, for labor brings happiness, we have seen, only when it contains cycles "of exhaustion and regeneration, of pain and release from pain." In order to be a perfect opposite to labor, work would have to effect an active resistance not only to the greater biological rhythms of earth and weather and growth but to interior organic urges also. *The Human Condition* does not describe work in that manner. The experience the author associates with work has far more of expressiveness, I would say, than of austerity, besides constituting a somewhat arrogant assault on nature: it is the experience of violence against natural things, the experience of human strength. The laborers, enduring their pain and exhaustion, would actually seem closer to the ascetic model than this is. Any element of asceticism attending the life of work that *The Human Condition* depicts would consist in a negative fact: that the workers do not go with the biological process within them. I doubt that this renunciation on their part is in Arendt's mind an especially deliberate and active one. Yet I would propose that her thesis gets some of its power from its implying the severity of the break that humankind within the world makes with its more spontaneous, quickly available organic forces such as physical emotion and the urge immediately to discharge physical energy. The act of work itself—or, for that matter, of "labor" in the producing of consumables—offers innumerable specific instances of that break. We could then put to a productive activity such questions as these: is it done with difficult skill painstakingly learned; what mental operation is involved; does the activity proceed by complex judgments or exact timings that are in combat with impulse?

I think especially of the commentary *The Human Condition* makes on the machine. Departing from the tradition that condemns the machine for being the foe of nature, the author accuses it of so perfecting the biological, laboring process as to plunge mankind the more deeply into biology. The machine reproduces the rhythms of labor, thereby closely enforcing the movements of its attendants; and it accelerates the more general biological movement toward consumption and the dissolving of things into consumables. But because the labor they require is on its way to losing all elements of pain and effort, the modern means of production fail to provide even the fullness of the organic, cyclical experience appropriate to labor.[2] Here is a fresh manner of thinking about the perennial question of the machine as a cultural event. Modern technology is put in the position of having to seek its defense in the claim usually advanced by its romantic detractors, that it does indeed go against organic spontaneity. I suspect that the defense can be made, at least for difficult professions and for other kinds of technical work demanding exact calculation in the handling of complicated materials; but this would mean that instead of considering the larger relationships between the machine and laboring or consumption we look to specific ways in which particular technical operations are encountered and experienced.

The most important fact of the artificial world, the fact for which the worker has made the foundations, is for Arendt the existence of a public whose members engage in action (to be distinguished from the more comprehensive term *activity*) and speech (words intended to persuade an audience, or to accompany action, rather than to form themselves into

2. Ibid., pp. 113–15, 128.

a durable art object). The model is the *polis*, the Greek city: *On Revolution* (1963) elects for councils, for American town meetings, the clubs and municipal bodies of the French revolution, the revolutionary *Räte* in Germany at the end of the first World War, the original Soviets of the Russian revolution, the councils in revolutionary Hungary in 1956—all of them bodies in which a politics was possible. *On Violence* (1970) finds the same political principle to suggest itself in the idea of participatory democracy as the New Left has revived it.[3]

In the genuinely political communities, individuality and the public are interdependent and exactly poised. Individuality is the purpose of the politics Arendt defines, the life of action and speech played out before a public. The action and speech reveal the "who" of the actor or speaker, as opposed to the "what." This "who" is the uniqueness of the individual, and it is expressed in the freshness of his action; it is not the sum of his aims and motives, however virtuous, for these he shares with others.[4] While the worker has a public of sorts in the market, where he displays his goods in order not only that they can be purchased but that his workmanship will bring him esteem,[5] he is something other than a fully political citizen, since he does not reveal himself in speech and action. The author says much about the differ-

3. Hannah Arendt, *On Revolution* (New York: The Viking Press, Viking Compass Edition, 1965), pp. 60, 238, 242–43, 261, 265–71; Hannah Arendt, *On Violence* (New York: Harcourt, Brace and World, 1970), p. 22.

4. *The Human Condition*, pp. 161, 184–85.

5. Ibid., p. 141.

ence between action and work, but the most striking point is that the meaning and honor of the worker's effort, the scale of his revealed selfhood, will always be limited to the dimensions of the things he produces, whereas the "who" that is revealed in action remains greater than anything the actor does; action does not threaten to limit it.[6]

The categories work and action are strong instruments of analysis. To perceive the difference between work, performed possibly in solitude, limited by the specifications of the task, and a "political" deed involving risk and courage and the progressive revealing of a public person in the presence of crisis is to discover something about the meaning of nobility. It should constitute no infringement on the categories themselves to suggest that in concrete activity work and action are inextricably compounded—as are labor and work, and labor and action. More particularly this should be the case if I am right in extending Arendt's idea of work to make it constitute a concept of interior as well as exterior resistance to organic impulses. Then much of what a civilization does, from the meticulous touches of a watchmaker to the decisions statesmen make in defiance of their political safety, derives some of its significance from its establishing, both within and outside the performers, an artificial world in the midst of organic existence.

Individuality, the aim of Arendt's politics, can happen according to her only in a real community of individuals aware of one another and engaged in in-

6. Ibid., pp. 160–61, 189–90.

teraction, not a society of laboring organisms, each caught separately within the pulse of life. Individuality by this idea needs a public for the obvious purpose of being observed and of having a group of people with whom it can interact. But the public individual is communal also—and more deeply, we might think—in his distinctive activity of making promises and forgiving. These, *The Human Condition* explains, preserve for the political citizen a freedom that action itself paradoxically threatens. An action and its results, in their endless unfolding, lead irreversibly to things the actor had never intended; it is only the willingness of others to forgive him for these that releases the citizen from enslavement to that irreversibility. The future is unpredictable; the ability possessed by the public person to make and keep promises gives him direction and identity, saves him from the effect of unpredictability. Promising and forgiving are densely public acts; unlike "Platonic rulership, whose legitimacy rested upon the domination of the self," a relationship the person has with himself, they depend on experiences that are founded completely in "the presence of others." Forgiveness, moreover, is itself an action, leaping up as freshly and unexpectedly as other human deeds.[7]

Arendt's public is a community also in its practice of a peculiarly public faculty, that of judgment and taste. A helpful essay here is "The Crisis in Culture," included in the collection *Between Past and Future* (1961, 1968). The simplest way of describing

7. Ibid., pp. 208–14, 216, 222.

judgment, or more particularly aesthetic judgment, as belonging to the *polis* in the author's terms is to point out that it addresses itself especially, though we might imagine not exclusively, to a class of artifacts belonging to her fabricated, public world—the art objects that, while they are made in private, fulfill themselves only in appearing before a public and in making the world beautiful. But judgment as "The Crisis in Culture," drawing on Kant as well as on Greek thought, defines it is more deeply political in the way it operates. Judgment, the essay argues, cannot legitimately act in private, bound to the idiosyncrasies of the individual. It is validated when the individual puts himself in the place of others who are judging the same object. And the communicating of judgment is not only a means of validation but a sharing of a common world, revealed to "common sense." It results in a common decision as to how this world is to look. The manner in which judgment speaks to judgment is not the philosophical mode of proving, because judgment does not deal with absolute truth. Its mode, rather, is that of persuasion, of what Kant called a "wooing" of others to consent; and persuasion comes close to the kind of address that the Greeks considered the typically political form of talk among citizens. And taste and judgment display the "who" of the judge.[8] Though this last comment especially would serve to distinguish the citizen judge from the workers, and a remark in *The Human Condition* that work produces in accordance

8. Hannah Arendt, "The Crisis in Culture," in *Between Past and Future: Eight Exercises in Political Thought* (New York: The Viking Press, 1968), pp. 218, 220–26.

with images or models exterior to the fabricator [9] might indirectly enforce the differentiation between work and judgments in taste, we should not be stretching the matter too far if we were to consider the disciplined shaping of a judgment, and its further articulation into persuasive words, as a craftsmanlike act, resembling in some senses the fashioning of an object. The important point about the essay for our purpose, though, is its revealing that the political community is also a sensitive community of taste.

This idea of taste and judgment provides some interesting comparisons with the notions of taste offered by the Agrarians—I am thinking here not of the New Critical devices for the examination of literature, but of the more common and daily taste the Agrarian citizen exercises. "The Crisis in Culture" discusses a judging that happens in public, and communicates itself by the public form of discourse that persuasion constitutes. Ransom's formal citizen can appreciate privately, and is a bit more humble before the object, allowing it to reveal itself on its own particular and beautiful terms. And the Agrarians, some of whom could be so strict in standards of literary criticism, would in other things encourage more fluency and circumstantiality in taste than is provided for, explicitly at least, in "The Crisis in Culture." The taste they indicate can respond to people, made objects, and nature whenever and however these present themselves, and it can refresh its feeling for land and nature not only by observation but by the labors of farming, without losing its courteous intelligence and independence.

9. *The Human Condition*, pp. 123–24.

We have left to look at the place within the human situation that Arendt assigns to love. *The Human Condition* does not set it directly within the community of politics. As a passion, we read, love destroys the worldly "in-between" that relates the citizens to one another and at the same time separates them.[10] The valid domains of love are elsewhere: one virtue of privacy, *The Human Condition* observes, is that love can exist in it, while love is "extinguished, the moment it is displayed in public."[11] Yet we can find references that would lead to another interpretation of love. A passage in "What Is Freedom?," an essay in *Between Past and Future*, discovers in the New Testament "an extraordinary understanding of freedom, and particularly of the power inherent in human freedom," the human capacity correspondent to that power being not "will" but "faith." This freedom, this acting out of faith, is expressed in "miracles"—in events that break in upon the normal and expected.[12] This definition of Gospel freedom and miracle is close to the definition the author generally relates to "action," the doing of a fresh deed; and action is for her the mode of the political citizen. In *The Human Condition*, in fact, she says that action is "the one miracle-working faculty of man"; and she describes the forgiveness preached by Jesus as being a fresh and miraculous action.[13] And if we may reasonably identify the forgiveness and the miracles of

10. Ibid., pp. 217–18.
11. Ibid., p. 47.
12. *Between Past and Future*, p. 168.
13. *The Human Condition*, pp. 216, 222.

faith with the miracles of love, then love of this kind has entered the realm of action and freedom.

In a number of ways the categories in *The Human Condition* could be made to bear on that love. The love that is associated with the miracle of grace can be pictured as having the look neither of the artifice the workers apply against nature nor of the decisions the citizens make, but of an extreme, nearly unconscious simplicity—a simplicity almost suggesting natural impulse and the unwilled rhythms of nature, though it is synonymous neither with biology nor with the civic world. But this character of acting love, differing apparently from the character of actions in the *polis*, may have some correspondence. Action, freedom mean for Arendt something other than a teeth-gritting strain of the will—in "What Is Freedom?" she argues against locating freedom in the will. Action in its freshness, if my reading of her gives me a right image of it, will seem, at least to the spectator, to spring instead from some spontaneous though not unconscious source. And just as we can ally the freedom of faith and love with "action" in this odd, contradictory ease—"naturalness," almost— that is an element of both, we could ally that freedom on the other hand with the "artifice" that marks the *polis*, if "artifice" be given the more general signification of resistance to human as well as outer nature. From one point of view the advent of love is the extreme assault on the instinctual and biological, more violent than is the wrenching of materials from nature, which may come easily enough of pleasurable skill, or the self-disciplines that pride and the desire for self-cultivation may dictate, or the pub-

110

lic heroic actions that can spring from exuberant energy. And if love has the interior force of passion, its conduct is disciplined and reflective. My aim here is not to give a definition to that love that would domesticate it to the more manageable human world, against which it witnesses, or to attribute to the normal, civic virtues an exaltation they cannot claim, but to find points of similarity or intersection.

❊   ❊   ❊   ❊

Theodore Roszak, like other cultural radicals of our time, continues a long critical tradition that demands the retrieval of the nature from which our willed and artificial world has alienated us. Human participation in nature as Roszak describes it is not merely—though it is partly—like the merging of ourselves with pulsing biological existence that *The Human Condition* speaks of; it is also a disciplined act of intellect and imagination. To conceive of the engagement in nature as being mental as well as carnal is of course not in itself distinctive. But Roszak's work has fresh and independent features. A sympathizer, albeit a carefully critical one, with the phenomenon that his *The Making of a Counter Culture,* which appeared in 1969, helped to define, he is in agreement with the emphasis that experiment in cultural rebellion has placed on the clamorous life of the senses; he argues that the richest consciousness is that which is most fully grounded in the physical and sensuous universe. But he comes closest to a more embracing

ural universe; and he claims that the combat the Western religions have waged against idolatry, mistakenly assuming that the "idolators" identified the object with the power revealed through it, set the West on its way to its modern perception of the universe as lifeless matter and dimension to be exploited.

Some of this—the complaint, at least, that we have lost contact with the wisdom and the rhythms of the flesh, fled from its wetness and swarminess—sounds a good deal like a call to that surrender to biology that Arendt treats of. But that would be a misconstruction of Roszak's thought. His interest is in states of consciousness that are lucid, precise, and ethical. *The Making of a Counter Culture* at one point contrasts the promiscuity in drugs that was then a mark of the counter culture with the careful, disciplined exploration that earlier experimenters had conducted into their own drug-induced experience—Roszak even makes a tentative appeal here to scientific discipline.[16] He likes the strain of mysticism in Jewish prophesy, George Fox, Blake, Tolstoy, Gandhi, that turns active rather than passive and brings its impassioned ethical vision to the world.[17] The stress throughout is not on the controls that organism should exercise over us but rather on the power of the whole consciousness, founded in organism, to perceive patterns in the universe beyond the purely

16. Theodore Roszak, *The Making of a Counter Culture: Reflections on the Technocratic Society and Its Youthful Opposition* (Garden City, New York: Doubleday and Company, Anchor Books, 1969), pp. 156–59.
17. *Where the Wasteland Ends,* p. 95.

rational ones, and to shape its experiences into intricate poetry.

Roszak's civilized ideas about the proper relationship between mankind and organic nature, it is clear, are sharply alternative to another notion that has made its occasional appearance, articulate or half formed, within counter-cultural radicalism—that we ought to plunge into what has been perceptively called a "biological soup," in which even morality loses its definiteness and becomes an essentially erotic urge to participate in community. But while Roszak wants intellectual discipline and ethical purposefulness, while the universe as he perceives it has differentiation and he would wish us to experience the unabstract, distinct things that inhabit it, he is hostile to the divisions and distances that he finds modern science and technology to effect within it: the division between self and Out There, and between mind and body. Modern science, of course, means for him the discipline of contracting the consciousness away from what is to be observed, so that the observation can be impersonal; and twentieth-century technology would then be, in effect, the brutal aggression that the contracted consciousness wages against the alienated Out There.

Roszak's scientists endow the universe with only one character that might be termed aesthetic, that of "objective quantity: size, variety, complexity of mechanism, vastness of space and time";[18] in other respects they probe and manipulate it with indifference. Charles Gillispie—whose work in the history of

18. Ibid., p. 198.

science, which gains Roszak's respect, finds the essence of modern science to lie in its severe discipline to objectivity—has depicted a posture toward objective reality on the part of some scientists that would appear to be almost exactly opposite to one of aggressive arrogance, an attitude of attentive submission to the unbending terms of objective truth. Roszak has doubted, of course, that completely objective knowledge of this sort in fact is achievable; but we should be safe in saying of Gillispie's scientists, as Roszak says of his, that the objectifying mentality is indeed possible.

Roszak's views about the states of mind that go with the objectifying of nature and the fracturing of experience are subject to other modifications. He might himself agree, for instance, that the complex and ordered consciousness he prizes in such manifestations as the poetry of Blake and the romantics involves the difficult action of an observing and analytical intelligence, painstakingly bringing shape to unformed sentiment. And if intellect and the will to order and precision must gain some autonomy within us, may we not discover in the angular, metallic features of the modern technological environment some dignity for being distillations of those virtues, however much they may also be distillations of insensibility and pride?

Most broadly we may question whether the experience of oneness is, as Roszak assumes, always richer than the experience attendant upon division. Denis de Rougemont's studies of religion and consciousness argue that the Western consciousness has its own richness precisely in its sustaining within itself, under the guidance of its religious traditions, paradoxical relationships among opposites and things separate: it has believed itself committed to live in the flesh and by the spirit; the love inculcated by Christianity establishes the uniqueness and integrity of the person loved, and the separateness of that person evokes the uniting love. My more limited suggestion is that the distancing of nature from us could be the occasion for a distinctive sensibility toward nature. To conceive of nature as "out there" and at the same time have the startled recognition that we are continuous with it; to imagine it as quantity and dimension and at that moment realize that it also blazes with color; to probe it with scientific instruments, build highways over it, and in countless other ways experience its vulnerabilities that require the most delicate touch: surely all this must make for an awareness of nature not necessarily more intense than that of other peoples—not even, perhaps, as intense as theirs—but nonetheless sensitive and at its best loving.

Though Roszak contends that the Western religions have had a major part in our break with nature, his intuition that gifts lie around us, separated from us only by our prideful resistance to them, is shared by the Western religious consciousness. And his thought has an elegance and an urgency that enlist the reader on his side. We should in the end hesitate to defend the temper of modern science and technology very strongly against his attack. Whatever feelings for nature modern civilization may make available, it is not constrained from assault on nature by a pattern of ritual and of daily contact as other cultures are, and its more obvious character is that of aggressiveness against whatever it can analyze, transform, or cover with cement. Roszak is eloquent in telling us this and in suggesting the goods that await just beyond the steel barriers we have set up.

*   *   *   *

Paul Goodman, who had been for many years a philosopher of personal liberation and social change when the rebellions of the late sixties appeared, like Roszak maintained a critical independence of popular protest even when sympathetic to it, and kept the social issue within a larger setting. Goodman makes a good complement to Roszak. *Where the Wasteland Ends* points to the powers and mysteries of nature from which we have estranged ourselves; Goodman's work considers how to coax specific good things from our own natures and from our surroundings, artificial and natural. Goodman's loose commonsensical reasoning, addressing itself first to this point, then to that, accommodates the conflicting offerings of artifice and organism, autonomy and association, disciplined exactness and the play of curiosity, the rigors of good machinist and scientific workmanship and the impulses of the senses. Goodman wanted a porous, unfinished kind of community that has a place in it for all these things, putting itself together in somewhat the same casual way that his argument does.

Goodman's writing is very much a matter of par-

118

ticular points: he claimed to be most at home in thinking about a solution to some specific problem. If his arguments have a philosophical center, it is perhaps to be found in the species of Gestalt psychology that Frederick S. Perls, Ralph F. Hefferline, and Goodman have described in *Gestalt Therapy* (1951). The ruling assumption is that the individual awareness is continually at work trying, with lesser or greater daring and clarity, to shape its disordered milieu into sharp figures. Awareness operates in a "field" composed both of organism, with its needs and energies, and of the environment in all its offerings; awareness at a specific time is operating within some narrower context in the field. The figure, or Gestalt, can be an image, a graceful rhythmic movement, [19] or, I suppose, a moral code or a philosophy—anything that selects what at the moment are the most important and insistent elements of the field, setting them into some coherence and allowing them expression. You are therefore engaged in completing your universe; for the Gestalten, feeble or strong, make up existence insofar as you really know it. One of the simplest demonstrations in the study is the trick picture that can represent either of two things—a chalice or two faces looking at each other, for example—according to how your mind arranges the details into a whole. Perls, Hefferline, and Goodman think of mental health as being the ability to form bright,

19. Frederick S. Perls, Ralph F. Hefferline, and Paul Goodman, *Gestalt Therapy: Excitement and Growth in the Human Personality* (New York: The Julian Press, 1951), pp. 231–32.

strong, integrating figures and to go deftly from making one figure to making another, which is the same as an ability to play freely within the field, to allow the most urgent and robust forces of the organism and the environment to assert themselves and get vivid expression in a figure. Illness is roughly the same, I gather, as Freudian repression. The particular Gestalt therapy the authors propose employs experiments that will let the patient see how various and changeable things can be at his hands, how teeming are the forces within and surrounding him clamoring for attention; he can then choose and order them with intelligence and vigor.

One thrust of our authors' gestaltism is toward an activist politics. The reason is that gestaltism provides them with the basis for an attack on the rendering of the Reality-principle they find in wide use within the psychoanalytic profession—the idea of an external reality more or less ready-made, to which the deeper personal urges have to be subdued or adjusted. The political implication of this Reality-principle, argues *Gestalt Therapy*, is that a daring and imaginative politics is to be shunned, for politics usually identifies "reality" with the safe and narrow frameworks within which it is conducting itself at the moment.[20] But if reality is something you complete, both by casting raw existence mentally into Gestalt figures and by acts of making that are the physical equivalent of forming Gestalten, then you want a more venturesome political thought than the establishment can provide.

20. Ibid., pp. 393–94.

I think also that Goodman was true to his gestaltist convictions, intentionally or not, when he adopted the creed of anarchism. What he meant by the word, we shall see, is a little elusive; but his taste for a diverse, decentralized, fairly disordered society is in effect a taste for uncompleted situations, and for the varied materials the imagination and the physical energies like to play with, and work into completed shapes. This implies a sensibility to environments that a reader can get from Goodman's writings: a sense, as tactile in its own way as the one we have found in *I'll Take My Stand*, of your surroundings as a coarse and substantial thing for you to run your mind and hand over. An experiment in *Gestalt Therapy* involves taking an object as common as a pencil or as rich as a painting and trying different ways of experiencing it, discovering how various is its factuality—the grasp of the pencil wood on the graphite, the pattern formed by the empty spaces between the main shapes of the painting.[21]

Some of the more interesting possibilities of the ideas in *Gestalt Therapy* lie in two configurations, slightly but importantly differing—should we say, two Gestalt forms?—of the arguments. By one configuration, we find a largely unitary or confluent existence. By the other, existence becomes more fragmented and the self a partly separate being, the fragments join with difficulty and forcefulness, and community is a rough affectionate gathering of positive individuals. The two conceptions are quite compatible, and together suggest that especially attrac-

21. Ibid., pp. 64–66.

tive property of Goodman's own work, the broad embrace of contrasting goods and virtues.

Much of *Gestalt Therapy* indicates the gentler view of an unbroken cosmos. The authors do not want to draw a deep line between organism and environment. The points of strongest awareness, the points at which the Gestalten should be forming, the study calls "contacts," and we would suppose that the term refers to contacts between the organism and its surroundings. But no—"contacting occurs at the surface-boundary *in* the field of the organism/environment"; and, explain the authors, they choose this wording "rather than 'at the boundary between the organism and the environment,' because . . . the definition of an animal involves its environment"; "breather" presumes air, "walker" presumes "gravity and ground," and so forth.[22] Nor is the individual self an isolated, self-existent thing. "In contact situations the self is the power that forms the gestalt in the field; or better, the self *is* the figure/background process in contact-situations"; and since the self is not a fixed thing but the process of contacting, the center point of the awareness that is coming into being, the self increases and diminishes as contact situations come and go.[23]

It is the way the authors put the self to functioning, though, that appears to set it furthest away from a sharp-lined individuality. For self-control, self-conquest, "character," *Gestalt Therapy* has little use: these amount to a state at once of mad arrogance—

22. Ibid., p. 258.
23. Ibid., pp. 373–74.

the arrogance of the conqueror—and of locking up the forces and possibilities that look for realization.[24] The healthy self is spontaneous, which means being fully within the situation that is working itself out, both accepting and actively willing toward the forces trying to get themselves fulfilled.[25] *Gestalt Therapy* also affirms a condition apparently opposite to the spontaneous: the state of responsibility. Responsibility is "the filling out of a contract," a free committing of yourself to consistency in some task. It is a worthy condition, but it sets merely the terms within which creative spontaneity will operate in the specific task at hand. A poet, recognizing the need in a particular situation for the sonnet form, may "contract"—make an interior commitment, the authors may mean—to write one, and then will keep to the sonnet meter; but the poet's spontaneity creates the images, the rhythm, and the meaning.[26]

So we are in "fields" rather than a formal structure of facts or a collection of disparate details. Existence composes into the brilliant figures the awareness conceives. The self lives not in will but in spontaneity and in healthy cooperation with its surroundings. This does not give the full sense of *Gestalt Therapy*, or of Goodman's own writings in social and educational criticism. The other controlling impression is of the active and difficult struggle with which the self breaks through its achieved patterns and gropes toward some new Gestalt. We sense the fear

24. Ibid., pp. 362–68.
25. Ibid., p. 376.
26. Ibid., p. 383.

that may attend the destruction of the old habit; the inner conflict that the strong self accepts and attends to, for the conflict is the condition of growth; the messages suffering gives; the courage and bright deftness of aware selfhood as it forms its Gestalten.[27] Confluent existence, inner and exterior, hardens and fractures into myriad separate elements each with its own energies, and the self is in more tensed although ultimately cooperative relations with them, straining them into beautiful coherent figures. The individual acquires will of a sort, though as theorists of therapy Perls, Hefferline, and Goodman would be wary of a word suggesting the rigid posture that "will" implies.

These two readings of *Gestalt Therapy* derive equally from the controlling principle that we must be in loving engagement with things. The experiment with pencils and paintings can be described, after all, either as an exercise in easy reception of the objects or as a friendly aggression against them, the viewer standing apart and dissecting them into desirable morsels; but by either description, the aim is to know them in more affectionate intimacy. These dominant implications of *Gestalt Therapy*—that we are to flow with existence, that we are to have hard encounters with it, and that both modes must represent a loving community with things—also inform Goodman's separate works. They constitute about as close a connection between the gestaltist study and Goodman's other writing as it would be advisable to establish. The task of compelling his casual and wandering commentary into the exact terms of *Gestalt Therapy*,

27. Ibid., pp. 232–33, 356–59, 374.

or of catching him straying, would be to burden the gestaltist principles with a descriptive responsibility they need not bear, and to require of Goodman's thought a philosophical consistency that is not the real source of its vigor.

Goodman devoted much of his critical writing to education. He perceived in human nature a curiosity restless to explore an existence inexhaustibly inviting in its roughness and disorder: restless, in effect, to form Gestalten for it. He disliked much of the formal educational system, for he presumed that young minds do not have to be coerced into a taste for learning. Let them loose upon the world and they will demand to be taught. Education should be incidental. Children will learn cause and effect as their environment presents itself to them; their curiosity, if unimpeded, will make them ask all sorts of questions about humanistic things as well as utilitarian. The world should abound in teachers and in places of learning, but these should be of every category—practitioners of crafts to whom the young can attach themselves, schoolteachers drawn from society at large and conducting small groups of pupils, training centers in industry, little places on the order of think tanks in which older youths so inclined can pursue complex interests, even academic institutions. Anyone who has a knowledge of the work at hand and an ability to explain it can become a teacher on the spot; the character of the teaching arrangement can be determined by the circumstances.

All this may sound like being in a romantic tradition finding childhood to be quick with an intellectual and emotional life that needs only to be tended lightly along the lines of its spontaneous growth and protected from restraint and falsehood. Goodman protests in *New Reformation* (1970) against educational structures that, by rigidly channeling the energy and attention of the student and thereby inhibiting impulse and dreaming, also threaten initiative, imagination, and inventiveness, schooling that thwarts and wastes the whole range of passionate contradictory human qualities.[28] Such a summary by itself misses an important but elusive element in Goodman's thought. If he rejects much of the particular discipline that exists in the school, he does so not for some vision of a humanity returned to a joyous and unfettered innocence. The people he would look for will be tough and sophisticated, the denizens of modern cities as well as the countryside, precise workers who are moralists about their work, mature lovers who can be faithful in their love. One of his major complaints is against every kind of cheap and dishonest task the economy puts people to. He would even want, so it seems, a fairly bruising environment that will make you learn technical skills for coping with it, and discover what it is to live with pain, and what you are really fitted to do. Virtues of this sort Goodman would not place at some antithesis to spontaneity and free passion: he would desire an integrity and directness and sharp delineation of personality that will be expressive equally in quick honest affection and close honest skill.

Education, then, is to be a matter of plunging

28. Paul Goodman, *New Reformation: Notes of a Neolithic Conservative* (New York: Random House, Vintage Books, 1971), pp. 76–77.

into a varied, confusing, reasonably difficult environment, asking questions as curiosity raises them, imi-
tating parents and other elders at their work, trying
out this and that skill. Your world must be filled with
teachers, incidental ones and teachers by career, and
they must make themselves available to you. If you
are allowed access to environment and to teachers,
you are pretty well bound to learn what you need to
know. Goodman offers the learning of speech as an
example of this—a "stupendous intellectual achievement" that comes without formal schooling; and in
demonstration that our technical environment will
teach itself to its inhabitants, he presents three of his
friends, "inveterate dropouts," who can design computer circuits.[29]

Goodman's idea of the way learning happens, bit
by bit, in gravelly scrapes against a surroundings, a
good education being almost synonymous with the
development of a whole self, endows the process of
getting educated with a rough elegance. He puts at
the center of his story a courageous and moral figure,
the student—a person who looks a good deal like
Goodman himself in his own independent and multifaceted career—seeking vocation in something like
the religious sense, moving inquiringly about the environment testing skills of hand and intellect against
it, and always assuming the final responsibility for
acquiring an education. We are given a feeling for
what the interior of a good learning is. The teacher's
vocation, too, comes to new life: it is not a formal
purveying of a neatly delimited field, but a large risk-

29. Ibid., pp. 79, 92–93.

(1964), "ought to be on the moral virtues of science itself, both austere"—that makes a nice counterbalance to a purely pastoral and libidinous anarchism—"and liberating." *New Reformation* speaks of a basic scientific research "valuable in itself as a quality of behavior, honest, humble, discriminating, responsible, cooperative, unprejudiced, experimental, progressive"; modern technicians are to keep in mind that technology is "a branch of moral philosophy, with the criteria of prudence, efficiency, concern for remote effects, safety, amenity, perspicuity and repairability of machines, caution about interlocking, priorities determined by broad social needs." [30]

Technology defined in this way will do as a sample of the good human act as Goodman represents it. Technology requires precise workmanship, but not workmanship narrowed to the dimensions of a technically competent moralless task under orders. A technologist must conduct under the command of his conscience a more varied project, for which he combines his skillful handling of impersonal materials with whatever he has learned of the community, the ecological situation, and the longer sequences of cause and effect. Presumably Goodman would allow for a reasonable specialization of knowledge and skill. The point, I imagine, is that the technologist must bring within his sphere of awareness and action as large a slice of the social as well as the more strictly "technical" side of the project as he

---

30. Paul Goodman, *Compulsory Mis-education,* published with *The Community of Scholars* (New York: Random House, Vintage Books, 1964), p. 11; *New Reformation,* pp. 42, 44.

can, whether by performing independently or by associating himself with knowledgeable colleagues. The moral argument for this is obvious enough; but other elements in Goodman's thought also come to mind. We can imagine that the technologists who follow his prescription look much like his questing student: independent beings, keeping their curiosity and intelligence alive by the variousness of their surroundings, of their knowledge, and of their activity, never relinquishing an item of moral or intellectual choice that they can hold to, sustaining the same total engagement with their environment that the student does.

Goodman's community would be a community of workers, and the freedoms he would insure for it will be, in large measure, freedoms for honest, independent work. The technical plant, for example, would get broken down into groups of workers that allow every participant some initiative—an initiative, Goodman insists, that should increase the ingenuity and effectiveness of the work. In *New Reformation* Goodman makes a point of being a conservative as well as a radical, and sets as his ideal a society all tangled with specific freedoms, with guilds and other particular communities—all these things together rendering the larger social community more diverse, interesting, and free. He would have each vocation stay by its ethic: teachers must honor information students tell them in confidence, technicians are to turn down socially harmful work, and so on. An activity that engages the taste and skill and commitment of the person performing it will not necessarily coincide with a paying job, and should not need to do so. In recommending a mixed economy on the Scandinavian order, containing different sorts of public and private institutions, Goodman suggests adding a sector of "pure communism" providing a "decent poverty for those who do not want to make money or are too busy with nonpaying pursuits to make money (until society gets around to overwhelming them with the coin of the realm)." [31]

Education, work itself, work in community as Goodman's writings prescribe them: all are presumably expressions in some sense of the human nature that is described in *Gestalt Therapy*. The idea of "nature" in Goodman's usage can have the contradictoriness that it often takes on when it means at the same time that-which-is and that-which-ought-to-be: Goodman acknowledged the problem and Roszak points it out in *The Making of a Counter Culture* in the course of an admiring chapter on Goodman.[32] Yet Goodman has given a sufficiently distinguishing notion of the vital, playful energies available to us; there is a good deal in them to imply the qualities Roszak locates in existence, though they can get themselves satisfactorily completed in small workaday experiences.

Occasionally Goodman will describe a nature that seems somewhat more "objective." He will talk, for instance, of physical nature. "To simplify the technical system and modestly pinpoint our artificial intervention in the [natural] environment" is his formula for a wise technology.[33] It is very much in the

31. *New Reformation*, p. 149.
32. *The Making of a Counter Culture*, pp. 195–97.
33. *New Reformation*, pp. 12–14.

spirit of Goodman: allow no one thing to dominate; draw on whatever is available; take health and plenteousness from nature, even as you practice your human skills. Nature also means in Goodman's writing a "nature of things." This simple phrase, referring to a preformed, independent reality, opens a problem if it is set beside the thesis Goodman and his colleagues present that much of reality consists of the Gestalten the self forms. We could meet the difficulty fairly easily by formulas distinguishing between the basic fixed potentialities of the self and the environment and the great range of Gestalten these permit; but it may be more useful simply to recognize that Goodman's respect for the "nature of things" accords with the principle in *Gestalt Therapy* of a loving commerce with what is around us. And if Goodman's objective nature is demanding as well as beneficent, requiring of the technologist modesty and precise workmanship, nature in *Gestalt Therapy* is comparably exacting with the self that maneuvers nature's restless materials into patterns.

There is a nature of things, *New Reformation* proposes—the cosmos does work dependably; and that book laments the state of those young New Leftists who, in their conviction that knowledge is manipulated by the establishment, can come to doubt that in our society simple, trustworthy facts are available.[34] I like to imagine this nature of things as giving all sorts of contours and supports to the universe Goodman perceives: guaranteeing that existence will be steady and reliable, a safe ground for a casual so-

34. Ibid., p. 48.

cial anarchism; providing objective truth that people can agree about, and in their agreement draw together in common trust and discourse; supplying a hard demanding factuality that technicians and other workers can submit to with exactness, humility, and honor.

Another kind of factuality with which Goodman's anarchist society can steady itself is the cultural heritage. He insists, against an apparent rejection of the past on the part of the New Left, that high literature, the arts, accumulated knowledge all be taken seriously—that humankind not attempt to begin its wisdom and lore all over again with each generation. But he does not establish a polarity—on this side, our petty lives, and over there, the High Culture of the past—and demand our obedience to the frozen perfect High Culture, which will save us. Instead he implicitly presents that culture as coming into being like the rest of the human product, by specific acts of workmanship (great ones, to be sure: he is no leveler on the matter), and in response to experiences and needs that we share with the artist. What we do in consulting the novel or painting, Goodman might have said, is to hold a conversation within the wider community of work and talk stretching over the centuries.

In Goodman's strong compound of imagination and common sense one element is lacking or no more than elusively present, a consciousness that human nature is the enemy as well as the ally of virtue, that civilization needs not free expressiveness only but a dialectic between expressiveness and disciplines resistant to it. Critical of centralized authority, *New Reformation* does not explore equally the possibilities within smaller and homelier groups for oppression of the powerless. The local community in the United States has failed to distinguish itself for racial justice, which was won in some measure when the Federal bureaucracy began breaking down with its uniform and uncommunal rules the old local arrangements. *New Reformation* observes that local liberty cannot alone suffice,[35] and Goodman's thought looks also, of course, to liberty for the professions; yet professions and guilds could prove a dubious repository for the rights of dissenters and nonmembers. Goodman's answer to the problem of oppression would to a large extent be to set up more communities, to break down the human mass into smaller and smaller particles, and shelter each from the rest of society. But this is not to subdue the final threat to my liberty—myself; a threat that I suspect Goodman was strongly aware of, for he looked at things and people toughly.

Here, I think, Goodman missed dwelling on a major function of the formal school: to liberate the mind by the method of presenting it with ideas, disciplines, and intellectual habits that may not be impulsively "natural" or, at first taste, pleasing to it. Goodman wanted the environment to do something like that; but can we expect from the world outside the school the sharpness of conflict among ideas precisely defined, the training in introspection and self-criticism; will the streets alone provide the young apprentices to life with the incessant knowledge and study of real and fictional alternatives to the existence they are familiar with?

The treatment Goodman favors for social and in-

35. Ibid., pp. 182–84.

dividual ills is to tap deeper into the personality and release its imprisoned forces. It is his notion of what those forces are, how they get self-awareness and expression, how rigorous and dignified is their task, that gives his world its toughness. Possessing a probing intellect as well as playful feeling, workmanlike sobriety along with impulsiveness, responsibility in passion rather than abandon, Goodman's individual pursues a lifelong project of self-education and self-making, carefully, observantly, never falling back upon a collective emotion. The community builds itself from the individual upwards. "Every pacifist career," Goodman writes of his son Matty, "is individual, a unique balance of forces, including the shared hope that other human beings will become equally autonomous. Most people want peace and freedom, but there are no pacifist or anarchist masses."[36] Here may be a clue to the meaning of the phrase "anarchism" in Goodman's use. I find no evidence in his writing of much interest in how, or whether, the state will wither away: he describes the progress of anarchism as lying in a series of piecemeal victories, one freedom after another gained,[37] and this gives an image of a good society packed and richly cluttered with professions and liberties, but it is not clear whether these can sum up by themselves into a sort of government, or must depend on government for their protection, or can exist outside the state and its methods. And if anarchism comes of personal, interior decision, then anarchism is right here, right now,

36. Ibid., p. 177.
37. Ibid., pp. 159–60.

in anyone who, in peace and self-discipline, decides to withdraw from mental servitude to institutions and collective mentalities, electing instead to pursue private taste and skill and conscience, and to join with others in affection and cooperative work. How wide a range of laws and institutions such a person will acquiesce in for the sake of convenience and social harmony becomes a secondary question: he or she is free of their ultimate command, ready for civil disobedience or peaceful sabotage when conscience requires. I believe that this understanding of anarchism would have gotten the assent of Goodman, who would dislike armed revolution for its violence and its tendencies toward a mass mind and mass emotions.

There, possibly, is the most imposing note in Goodman's writing: his call to a life of reflective, courageous, and warmhearted individuality. We can think immediately of the innovative, dissenting existence Goodman himself led. His community centers in the individual, who sustains it by conscious acts. Still, it has a power of its own to nourish its members, if they are mindful of its offerings.

AFTERWORD

A good portion of these essays has been taken up with the uses and the inherent dignity of the drier or "harder" virtues: exact workmanship, the disciplines of courtesy and poetry, the inner check. I have tended to seize on passages in my authors' works that could be made out to isolate those virtues as a distinct order of experience. These choices on my part constitute an instance of the very problem that informs this study. It is a problem that is certainly central within Christianity, I suspect important for Judaism, and perhaps at least implicit in other faiths. It is this: is there an acceptable "pride" within human affairs that is not synonymous with the pride condemned by theology, a legitimate seeking for self-vindication under circumstances of effort and discipline, with the attendant risks to the more receptive and more celebrative side of life?

The most affirmative answer within a Judeo-Christian tradition could be no more than hesitant and qualified. The essential qualification within the writings that have been our formal subject is that the colder virtues are usually put into association with something outside or beyond them—the reverence on which rests the moral sternness of Carlyle's heroes, the poetic sensibility that Tate and Ransom place in the care of poetic technique. And the safest strategy for their defense, of course, is to find what services they may have to offer, by way of contrast or complication or refinement, to the richer and more generous experiences.